English Leaders of Religion

EDITED BY A. M. M. STEDMAN, M.A.

CARDINAL NEWMAN

English Leaders of Religion.

UNDER the above title MESSRS. METHUEN propose to publish a series of short biographies, free from party bias, of the most prominent leaders of religious life and thought in this and the last century.

CARDINAL NEWMAN.	*R. H. Hutton.*
JOHN KEBLE.	*W. Lock.*
CHARLES SIMEON.	*H. C. G. Moule.*
BISHOP WILBERFORCE.	*G. W. Daniell.*
JOHN WESLEY.	*J. H. Overton.*
F. D. MAURICE.	*Colonel F. Maurice.*
THOMAS CHALMERS.	*Mrs. Oliphant.*

Other volumes will be announced in due course.

DR. NEWMAN.

(From an engraving published about the year 1850.)

CARDINAL NEWMAN

BY

RICHARD H. HUTTON

London

METHUEN AND CO., 18, BURY STREET, W.C.

1891

PREFACE.

THE whole of this little essay was written and in type, and most of it corrected for the press, before Cardinal Newman's death. I thought it better, considering the smallness of the space available for the treatment of so great a subject, to devote the main part of the book to the study of Dr. Newman's life before leaving the Anglican Church,—in other words, to the course of thought which led him to the Church of Rome,—and to compress the latter part of his career into a single long chapter. This seemed to me the best way of making the book of interest to the great majority of English readers.

R. H. H.

CONTENTS.

CARDINAL NEWMAN.

CHAPTER I.

HIS GENUINENESS AND GREATNESS.

IT is a strange and not a discreditable characteristic
of the days in which we live, that, in spite of the ardour
with which the English people have devoted themselves
to material progress and the scientific studies which
have ministered to material progress, one man at least
has been held to be truly great by the nation, who has
crossed all its prejudices and calmly ignored all its
prepossessions; who has lived more than half his life
in what Protestants at least would call a monastery,—
for his home at Littlemore as well as at Edgbaston
was more than half monastic,—who has loved penance,
who has always held up the ascetic life to admiration,
who has haunted our imaginations with his mild and
gentle yet austere figure, with his strong preference
even for superstition as compared with shallow, optimistic
sentiment; and has impressed upon us even more by
his practice than by his teaching, that "the lust of the
flesh, and the lust of the eyes, and the pride of life, are

B

not of the Father but of the world." Cardinal Newman
has not been the more popular for being a Cardinal,
but the Church of Rome has certainly been less
unpopular in England since a man of such plain and
simple life as he, was ranked among the princes of the
Roman Catholic Church.

I suppose that one may safely regard it as a standard
of true greatness to surpass other men of the same
calibre of culture and character, men with whom comparison is reasonable, in the ardour and success with
which any purpose worthy of the highest endeavour is
prosecuted. Measuring by this standard, it would be
hard to fix on any man now living in England who
could rival Cardinal Newman in the singleness, the
devotion, the steadfastness, and the nobility of his main
effort in life. I say this, though I cannot adopt for myself his later conception of the Church of Christ, hardly
even that earlier conception which led so inevitably to
the later. But that is nothing to the purpose. What
is perfectly clear to any one who can appreciate Cardinal
Newman at all, is that from the beginning to the end
of his career he has been penetrated by a fervent love
of God, a fervent gratitude for the Christian revelation,
and a steadfast resolve to devote the whole force of a
singularly powerful and even intense character to the
endeavour to promote the conversion of his fellow-
countrymen, from their tepid and unreal profession of
Christianity to a new and profound faith in it,—which
new and profound faith in it could, in his belief, be
gained only by the reorganization of the Christian
Church, and its re-enthronement in a position of authority
even greater than that which it held in the middle
ages. I know that this conception of Cardinal Newman

as having devoted a singularly large and apprehensive intellect to the pure purpose of re-Christianizing a half-Christian, or less than half-Christian, people, is not frankly accepted by some of his keenest critics. Professor Huxley, for instance, has said quite lately,[1] " If I were called upon to compile a Primer of Infidelity, I think I should save myself trouble by making a selection from these works" (namely, Cardinal Newman's Tract 85 in the *Tracts for the Times*, and the *Essay on the Miracles recorded in the Ecclesiastical History of the Early Ages*), "and from the *Essay on Development*, by the same author." I do not suppose that Professor Huxley meant to suggest that these essays of Dr. Newman were written with the intention of undermining belief, though he thinks them so admirably adapted for that purpose. But unquestionably there is a very wide-spread suspicion, which I suppose Professor Huxley shares, that Cardinal Newman has all through his life been on the very brink of infidelity, and only saved from it by the deliberate exercise of a strong and sturdy *will* to believe. For my part, I utterly reject this view, and do not think that it can for a moment be held by any one who carefully studies and appreciates his career,—which very few of his critics do, Professor Huxley least of all, as he shows by his astoundingly unintelligent criticism of a very significant and very just passage from the *Essay on Miracles*, which almost immediately follows this observation on the sceptical tendency of Dr. Newman's writings. To my apprehension, the true theory of Dr. Newman's attitude of mind through a long life is the passage in his *Apologia*

[1] In the *Nineteenth Century* for June, 1889 ; note on p. 948.

pro vitâ suâ (so often quoted unintelligently by Roman
Catholics who have never really discriminated between
difficulties and doubts), in which Newman said, that
" ten thousand difficulties do not make one doubt, as I
understand the subject; difficulty and doubt are incom-
mensurate; " [1] and which he illustrated by adding, " Of
all points of faith, the being of a God is to my own
apprehension encompassed with most difficulty, and
borne in on our minds with most power."   It might as
well be said, that because a man sees with the most
vivid and minute apprehension the difficulty of answering the necessitarian arguments against responsibility
and free will, or the difficulty of proving the existence
of any external world, he doubts the existence of his
own responsibility and free will,—though nothing else
in the world is so certain to him, not even the existence of the external world itself,—as that Cardinal
Newman's subtle and individual appreciation of the
various strong points of the sceptic's position, implies
any inclination to doubt the truth, and not only the
truth, but the certainty of the Christian revelation.

It is true, of course, that the greater part of Cardinal
Newman's life has been given to the discussion of the
question how such difficulties as beset the revealed
Christian theology ought to be met.   He himself has
told us that he began the study of this class of difficulties quite in his boyhood by reading Paine and David
Hume, and it is evident that no one ever entered into
these difficulties with more genuine insight—into what
they really prove and what they are really worth.   It
is just the same with a much more imposing class of

---

[1] *Apologia*, p. 374.

difficulties, the difficulties caused by the spectacle of
the world's worldliness, misery, and sin. In the celebrated passage in the *Apologia* which has been so often
quoted, the passage in which Dr. Newman contrasts
the moral scenery of the actual world with that which
he should have expected from his knowledge of the
Creator, whose holiness is to him the deepest of all
certainties—a certainty on a level with the certainty
of his own existence—he shows the same profound
apprehension of the obstacles with which the Christian
theology has to grapple, and the same absolute confidence that, however incompetent it is to solve these
difficulties, it can and will triumphantly surmount
them. This is what makes Cardinal Newman a really
great man. His whole life has been lived in the passionate confidence that these great, these apparently
appalling difficulties, are not only not really insuperable,
but are infinitely less than those which any man would
encounter who, dealing honestly with his own conscience,
should yet give up as false the belief in the Divine
origin of the world and the Divine character of Christianity. He has treated the difficulties of faith in his
own way, and I cannot but think, in relation to that
considerable class of them for the treatment of which
he relies absolutely on the authority of the Church, in
a very unsatisfactory way ; but he has never in the least
ignored them, and he has devoted extraordinary learning, genius, and ardour of nature, through a long life,
with the most perfect singleness of purpose, to the
battle with them. If any man ever succeeded in anything, Cardinal Newman has succeeded in convincing
all those who study his career with an approach to
candour and discrimination, that the depth and luminous-

ness of his conviction that the true key to the enigma of life is God's revelation of Himself in Christ and in His Church, are infinitely deeper in him, and more of the intimate essence of his mind and heart, than his appreciation, keen as it is, of the obstacles which stand in the way of those convictions and appear to bar the access to them.

Now if the greatness of a man depends, as I have said, chiefly on the ardour and energy which he devotes to adequate objects, Cardinal Newman's life has certainly been a very great one.   There are two lines of Wordsworth's—whose poetry, strange to say, never "found" Dr. Newman, though there is so much in his writings that seems like a paraphrase of some of Wordsworth's finest poetry—which delineate exactly the labour and strenuousness of the thinking aspects of his life—

> "The intellectual power through words and things
> Went sounding on a dim and perilous way."

This does not express that vividness of his faith in Divine guidance, that exultation in the wisdom and spiritual instinct of his Church, which has furnished him with his confidence, and guaranteed his success, but does exactly express the procedure of his intellect, as he has taken exact measure of the depths of the various channels by which he might safely travel to "the haven where he would be," the care with which he has buoyed the quicksands and the sunken rocks, and the anxious vigilance with which he has traced out the winding and often perilous passages in the way.   But how this aspect of his mind, how the results of his arduous, intellectual explorations which he has so fully and frankly given to the world, can have concealed from any man of large insight, the profound and passionate conviction which lay beneath all this delicate intellectual appreciation of difficulties, I cannot for a moment understand.   The very terms in which Dr. Newman states his apprehension of the difficulties imply the most unhesitating confidence that these difficulties will vanish utterly away when viewed in the full light of the Christian revelation.   Take the very first sermon of which there is any record amongst Dr. Newman's printed writings, one preached in Oxford in January, 1825, and entitled *Temporal Advantages,* when he can only have been twenty-four years of age, from the text, "We brought nothing into this world, and it is certain we can carry nothing out; and having food and raiment, let us be therewith content," and consider if it be possible that that sermon could have been written by a man who did not feel to the full depth of his heart and soul the reality and power of the Christian faith: "What can increase their peace who believe and trust in the Son of God?   Shall we add a drop to the ocean, or grains to the sand of the sea? . . . It is in this sense that the Gospel of Christ is a leveller of ranks; we pay indeed our superiors full reverence, and with cheerfulness, as unto the Lord; and we honour eminent talents as deserving admiration and reward; *and the more readily act we thus because these are little things to pay.*" [1] Here the utterly unworldly nature of the man, the vivid spiritual feeling that the inward life in God is everything of the smallest consequence to the soul, spoke out plainly, and at a time when Dr. Newman had not reached anything like the full maturity of his power.

[1] *Parochial and Plain Sermons,* vol. vii. p. 73.

From that date onwards the vividness of his spiritual insight grew steadily, till it reached its highest point, and was recognized generally by the world when he wrote his religious autobiography in 1864. Writing of his own boyhood, when he was only just a man, he said of himself, " I used to wish that the Arabian tales were true ; my imagination ran on unknown influences, on magical powers and talismans ; I thought life might be a dream and I an angel, and all this world a deception, my fellow - angels hiding themselves from me, and deceiving me with the semblance of a material world." And in the sermon on " The mind of little children " [1] he speaks professedly from his own experience when he says, " This we know full well—we know it from our own recollections of ourselves and our experience of children—that there is in the infant soul, in the fresh years of its regenerate state, a discernment of the unseen world in the things that are seen, a realization of what is sovereign and adorable, and an incredulity and ignorance about what is transient and changeable, which mark it as the first outline of the matured Christian, when weaned from things temporal, and living in the intimate conviction of the Divine presence."

I quote these passages only to show how completely the spiritual reality of the Oxford preacher had its roots in his own past, how certain it is that Newman was speaking from the depths of his own experience when he said, that from a very early age he had rested " in the thought of two, and two only, supreme and luminously self-evident beings, myself and my Creator." It is simply ridiculous for any one who knows intimately

---

[1] *Parochial and Plain Sermons,* vol. ii., Sermon vi.

the whole series of his writings to suppose for a moment that Newman's nature is sceptical, and his mind kept only by force of will from toppling over into unbelief. On the contrary, his nature is profoundly and entirely penetrated by the Christian idealism. And had it been otherwise, I believe that he would have been much more likely to ignore the sceptical aspects of the religious problems of the day altogether, instead of giving them so profound a study. It was his absolute confidence that nothing could shake his faith in the truth of revelation that induced him to master so completely as he did the various aspects of the objections which led so many men to withhold their faith from Christianity. This then I regard as one certain test of Cardinal Newman's greatness, that throughout a long life he has followed with singular tenacity and concentration of purpose one grand aim—that of winning his fellow-country-men from their tepid and formal Christianity to a Christianity worthy of the name, in spite of obstacles in the way which he has recognized with a candour and a vivacity that have strangely misled some of his critics into imagining that he appreciated even more the obstacles to belief than he did the spiritual power by which those obstacles were to be surmounted.

A second safe test of greatness is to be found in the unhesitating and unswerving consecration of great genius or talent—genius or talent of a calibre sufficient to detach a man from his original pursuit, and to secure him distinguished success in a different field of effort, —to the disinterested purpose with which he set out in life. It would be difficult to find a clearer case of this than is presented by Cardinal Newman's career. His literary power has been so great, and has shown itself in a style of such singular grace and charm, as well as in irony of such delicacy and vivacity, that the highest literary eminence was easily within his reach, had he cared to win it, long before his name was actually known to the world at large; and he would have been a great power in literature had he cared to devote himself to literature in the wider sense, before the Oxford movement had begun to cause anxiety in the Established Church. But power of this kind is precisely what he never coveted, or indeed, in his earlier years, was so much as conscious of his ability to attain.   It must have been some time before it dawned upon him that he had any such power at all.   Perhaps when in the early part of 1833 Hurrell Froude and he chose at Rome a motto for the *Lyra Apostolica* from the words of Achilles when returning to the battle, of which the drift was, "You shall know the difference now that I am back again," he had some inkling of his literary genius, as well as of his force of character.   But I think that the motto in question had much more reference then to his zeal than to his literary genius; and assuredly up to that time—when his history of the Arian heresy had not yet appeared—he seems to have shown no sort of consciousness of literary power, and to have hardly aimed, in his more serious work, at anything like literary form.   The history of the Arian heresy is a very clear and accurate but a very homely, not to say dry, theological discussion.   And for the next thirteen years at least, that is, from the thirty-second to the forty-fifth year of his life, it was only in a few short poems, and a few of the later University sermons, that he betrayed his strange mastery of literary effect.

All his many publications during this period of his life

are remarkable for a severe and business-like treatment
of the theological subjects with which he dealt.   It
was not indeed till after he became a Roman Catholic
that Dr. Newman's literary genius showed itself adequately in his prose writings, and not till twenty years
after he became a Roman Catholic that his unique poem
was written.   The verses in the *Lyra Apostolica* are
almost the only early evidence of his rare and vivid
imagination.   And as to that keen and searching irony
of which he was afterwards a master, there was little
trace of it till after he had nearly completed his
fiftieth year.   Now it is a striking test of his true
greatness, that these great literary gifts should have
remained in him all but latent for so long a period,
and yet not quite latent, for they must have revealed
themselves partially to himself in the remarkable though
brief poems of which he wrote so many during his
Mediterranean tour in 1833.   What it shows is, that
he really lost himself in his work of restoring, as he
thought, the Church of England, and, as it proved, of
convincing himself and a good many of his friends that
the only true Church was the Church of Rome.   But
what was strictly speaking missionary work absorbed
him so completely between 1833 and 1845 that he seems
to have had neither time nor care for the development
of his own literary powers, which he used almost without noticing them, and never used at all to the full
till after he had found his goal in Rome.   Yet the man
who had shown such exquisite and almost Æschylean
genius as is betrayed in his poem on *The Elements*,
and the weird analogy which he drew between the
Jewish people and the Greek Œdipus in the *Lyra
Apostolica*, cannot possibly have been quite ignorant

that there was in him a rich vein of literary power if he had only chosen to turn aside from his self-appointed task of restoring authority to the Anglican Church, to cultivate and exert it. I do not know any better test of true devotion to a mission than Dr. Newman showed in pouring out the *Tracts for the Times*, the lectures on *Justification*, or the essays elaborating the *Via Media*, as he called it, and the various and numerous contributions to Anglican divinity, with unremitting zeal, and without apparently the slightest regard for popular literary effect,—and this too for a long period of years, —after he had discerned in himself the power to write as he wrote in such poems as these :—

THE ELEMENTS (*A Tragic Chorus*).

Man is permitted much
To scan and learn
In Nature's frame ;
Till he well-nigh can tame
Brute mischiefs, and can touch
Invisible things, and turn
All warring ills to purposes of good.
Thus as a God below, he can control,
And harmonize what seems amiss to flow
As severed from the whole
And dimly understood.

But o'er the elements
One Hand alone,
One Hand has sway.
What influence day by day
In straiter belt prevents
The impious Ocean, thrown
Alternate o'er the ever-sounding shore ?
Or who has eye to trace
How the Plague came ?
Forerun the doublings of the Tempest's race ?
Or the Air's weight and flame
On a set scale explore ?

> Thus God has willed
> That man, when fully skilled,
> Still gropes in twilight dim ;
> Encompassed all his hours
> By fearfullest powers
> Inflexible to him ;
> That so he may discern
> His feebleness,
> And e'en for earth's success
> To Him in wisdom turn,
> Who holds for us the keys of either home,
> Earth and the world to come.

Yet I doubt if anything as powerful as that could
have been written under any other than a strictly religious inspiration.   At all events, there is no sign in
Newman's career of the general exercise of high imagination for any other than a strictly religious purpose.   It
seems to have been elicited in him by his religious aims,
and never to have been elicited by any other kind of
aim.   Would not Æschylus himself, if he had lived
again in our generation, have been proud to have
written the following on the Jewish race ?—

> " O piteous race !
> Fearful to look upon ;
> Once standing in high place,
> Heaven's eldest son.
> O aged blind,
> Unvenerable ! as thou flittest by,
> I liken thee to him in pagan song,
> In thy gaunt majesty,
> The vagrant king, of haughty-purposed mind,
> Whom prayer nor plague could bend ;
> Wronged at the cost of him who did the wrong,
> Accursed himself, but in his cursing strong,
> And honoured in his end."

There seems something appropriate in the fact, that
the man who wrote these poems, and many like them

in his youth, should yet never have sought, or apparently
have so much as thought of seeking, to cultivate his
literary faculty for its own sake at all, but should have
re-discovered it, as it were, from time to time, just when
it was most needed for the main purpose of his life.
His power of irony came out, for instance, for the first
time in its full strength in the *Lectures on Anglican
Difficulties*, and subsequently again in his *Lectures on
Catholicism in England*, but assumed perhaps its most
exquisite form in the short conversation in which he
summed up the drift of his controversy with Mr.
Kingsley on the supposed countenance which he had
given to the view that cunning, and not truth, is the
proper weapon of the Roman Catholic Church in her
dealings with the world. But in spite of his singular
command of imaginative eloquence, of the most rare
and delicate pathos, and of a satire finer at once in its
point and in its reserve than any satire of this generation,
Cardinal Newman has never apparently felt the slightest
disposition or desire to use these great gifts in any
cause at all except that to which he has dedicated his
whole life; and the finest bit of irony which he ever
penned he suppressed in later editions of his work.
Indeed, widely read as he is in general literature, there
are probably fewer references to that literature in
Cardinal Newman's writings (if we except perhaps the
lectures on *The Idea of a University*, where such references were almost essential), than in those of any third-
rate or fourth-rate theologian of his day. Perhaps the
only glimpse which the English world has had of his
purely literary tastes has been in the interest he has
taken in adapting the plays of Terence for the acting of
the boys of his Edgbaston school, and the skill with

which he has trained them to perform their parts on that little classical stage. But that was a mere fragment of his duties as head of a Roman Catholic school, in the administration of which he was concerned to show that the lighter play of children's minds was not to be neglected. For the most part, the long series of his works show very little trace indeed of the deep interest he takes in general literature, so completely has he subordinated all his thoughts and cares to the one great purpose of his life, and so averse has he been to allow himself to be even apparently diverted from the more serious of his tasks. I think there is hardly any other instance in our literature of so definite and remarkable a literary genius being entirely devoted, and devoted with the full ardour of a brooding imagination, to the service of revealed religion. For it has been definitely *revealed* religion, and no mere philosophy of religion, which has absorbed Cardinal Newman's attention from his earliest youth to his latest age. He has indeed thought much and subtly on the philosophy of faith, as a long series of his Oxford sermons, and the volume entitled *The Grammar of Assent*, sufficiently show. But with him the philosophy of faith has been purely subordinate to laying the foundation of faith in Christian doctrine and dogma, and not in one of those thin, speculative substitutes for a Christian creed which have so often been in vogue among rationalistic mystics. Whether tried then by the test of the nobility, intensity, and steadfastness of his work, or by the test of the greatness of the powers which have been consecrated to that work, Cardinal Newman has been one of the greatest of our modern great men.

CHAPTER II.

JOHN HENRY NEWMAN was born in London on the
21st of February, 1801. He was the son of Mr. John
Newman, a member of the banking firm of Ramsbottom,
Newman, & Co., who at one time lived near Blooms-
bury Square, in the garden of which John Henry
Newman and Benjamin Disraeli used to play together
about 1810. The bank failed soon after the peace of
1815 had caused the contraction of the paper currency
and the rapid fall of prices, and this made it necessary
for Newman to take his degree without reading for
honours, at the earliest possible age.

Mrs. Newman was a Miss Fourdrinier, a member of
a Huguenot family which had settled in London as
paper manufacturers, and had introduced some important improvements into the machinery of paper
making. She was a moderate Calvinist, and taught
her children to read and love Scott, Romaine, Newton,
Milner, and all sincere thinkers of that school. From
a child Newman was taught to take great delight in
the Bible, and to the effect produced on him by Scott's
essays and commentary, he declares that he may almost

be said " to owe " his " soul." It was Scott's " bold
unworldliness " and " vigorous independence of mind "
which so deeply impressed him. " He followed truth,"
says Dr. Newman, " wherever it led him, beginning with
Unitarianism, and ending in a zealous faith in the Holy
Trinity ;" and it was Scott who first planted deep in his
mind " that fundamental truth of religion." Indeed,
before he was sixteen he had made " a collection of
Scripture texts in proof of the doctrine," with remarks,
he believes, of his own upon them. And upon this
foundation, no doubt, was erected that firm faith in the
necessity of dogma as part and parcel of revelation
on which in later life he so often insisted. The two
principles which he borrowed from Scott as " the scope
and issue of his doctrine " were " Holiness before peace,"
and " Growth the only evidence of life." From the
time when, as a boy, he read Law's *Serious Call*,
Dr. Newman dates his firm inward assent to " the doctrine of eternal punishments as delivered by our Lord
Himself," in as true a sense as he held that of eternal
happiness, though, as he remarks, he has tried in
various ways " to make the truth less terrible to the
reason." When he was only fifteen he took great
delight in reading the extracts from the Fathers which
Milner gives in his Church history, and which prepossessed him in favour of the conceptions of ecclesiastical
influence and life which he found there, even at the
very time when he was induced to take up from Newton's
book on the prophecies, a notion so inconsistent with
the belief of the primitive Church, as that the Church
of Rome is Antichrist—a conception which for many
years, he declares, " stained " his imagination, even
after his intellect had given judgment against it.

And in the same year, the autumn of 1816, when he
was not yet sixteen, he was taken possession of by the
conviction that it was God's will that he should lead a
single life, a conviction which held its ground ever since
with certain brief intervals of a "month now and a month
then," up to the age of twenty-eight, after which it
possessed him without any break at all. Add to these
impressions, clearly not very coherent, since his admiration for the early Fathers was certainly wholly inconsistent with his belief that Rome was Antichrist, the
rather capricious doctrine which he borrowed from a
book of Romaine's, that men know whether they are elect
or not, and that, if elect, they are of course sure of
their "final perseverance,"—a view which he held till
a year or two after he had taken his degree at Oxford,
when it gradually faded away,—and we find enough
material for theological fermentation in his dreamy and
profoundly susceptible mind. His love of music and his
skill in it no doubt added to the charm of a somewhat
dreamy life.

Newman took his degree in 1820, a few months before
he completed his twentieth year, and, as I have said,
his name did not appear in the honours list at all, as
his graduation was hurried on in consequence of his
father's failure, which rendered it necessary that he
should, as soon as possible, be independent of external
aid. His early University life, of five or six years, was
spent at Trinity College, and he is said to have published
in 1821 two cantos of a poem on *St. Bartholomew's Eve*,
which I have never seen. No doubt the Huguenot
traditions in his mother's family rendered that event
one of the most impressive to him in all the range of
modern ecclesiastical history, and perhaps it is a matter

of some surprise that it did not prove to have exerted greater influence than it actually did, as an
antidote to his patristic prepossessions, especially in connection with Newton's teaching that Rome is Antichrist.

In 1823 Newman was elected to a fellowship in Oriel
College, then the most distinguished in the University.
It was at this time that he was most lonely, not having
as yet formed any close friendships in Oriel, and feeling,
as he says, rather " proud of his college " than at home
there. Dr. Copleston, who was at that time Provost of
Oriel, to whom Newman afterwards paid so fine a
tribute in his lectures on *The Idea of a University*, once
met him taking his lonely walk, and said to him with a
bow "Nunquam minus solus quam cum solus," a sentence which must always have described Dr. Newman's
feeling for solitude, though he soon formed an intimate
friendship with Dr. Pusey, which lasted to the end of
the latter's life, though it was, of course, more or less
broken in upon by Dr. Newman's conversion to Roman
Catholicism. In the same year he first read Butler's
Analogy, and gathered from it two principles, which, as
he tells us himself, profoundly influenced his future
course of thought. The one was that you should interpret the less certain aspects of what is called natural
religion, in the sense of revealed religion, and not *vice
versâ*, in other words, that you should take the sacramental system of revealed religion as the key to natural
religion, and look at material phenomena as intended to
convey, and actually conveying, spiritual influences.
This teaching perfectly fell in with his boyish dream that
the world was not what it seemed, and that a certain
disguise of higher influences under a material mask
might be involved in the structural principles of the

universe. And this teaching was confirmed later by Newman's profound love for Keble's *Christian Year*.

Keble was a fellow of his new College, and his volume of poems so entitled was published in 1827, when Newman was already beginning to exercise a considerable influence at Oriel as a tutor of his College and as an examiner in the University. The doctrine "that material phenomena are both the types and the instruments of real things unseen" was suggested by Butler's principle that there is a real analogy between the system of nature and the system of revelation, and that the latter should teach us to interpret the former rather than the former to interpret the latter, while Keble's poetry suggested a hundred ways in which that analogy might be traced.

The second principle which Newman learned from Butler was, that " probability is the guide of life." But he could not, as he tells us, accept this as satisfactory in the region of religious belief. If it were possible to act on such a principle, "the celebrated saying, ' O God, if there be a God, save my soul, if I have a soul,' would be a legitimate form of devotion; but," as Newman asks, "' who can really pray to a Being about whose existence he is seriously in doubt ?'" Might not the word "seriously" be omitted ? Who could really pray to a highly probable God, to a God for the reality of whose existence he thinks there are even ninety-nine chances against one ? Is it prayer till you recognize your mental contact with the object of prayer ? Indeed Newman felt this so strongly, and felt so profoundly the certainty of God's relation to himself, that he learned to draw a distinction between the reasons which he could give for any belief and the certainty with which he held it, holding that reasons which in themselves only amount to probabilities are often transformed into absolute certitude by the action of the Divine will. Thus Newman accepted Butler's teaching only so far as it displayed the rational *preparation* for belief, but rejected it so far as it suggested that any doubt as to the highest truths might remain.

During the earlier part of his life at Oriel College Newman made a fast friendship with Dr. Hawkins, afterwards the Provost of the College, and he attributes to the influence of Dr. Hawkins that finer care in the use of words, that delicacy in discriminating between cognate ideas, that habit " of obviating mistakes by anticipation, which to my surprise has since been considered, even in quarters friendly to me, to savour of the polemics of Rome." Dr. Hawkins was a fine scholar, and a scholar who was no more of a casuist than any man must be who is careful in distinguishing between different though closely related ideas. It seems to me that no greater mistake was ever made than in ascribing to the influence of Roman Catholic craft and casuistry that delight which Cardinal Newman has always taken in distinguishing between closely related yet quite different thoughts, and which he learned at Oxford, mostly from Dr. Hawkins, partly also from Dr. Whately. I am far from familiar with Roman Catholic controversy, but, so far as I know it, it seems to me to be rather deficient than prolific in the sort of subtlety which springs out of refined scholarship. Casuistic subtlety is one thing, and scholarly or psychological subtlety quite another. The former, which appears to be so abundant in the manuals of pastoral theology and morality, is a subtlety that has been organized for a particular practical purpose, and

which often ignores the most important differences
when that practical purpose is not in question. But
the sort of subtlety in which Dr. Hawkins and Dr.
Whately were very soon surpassed by their companion
and pupil was a very different thing—a subtlety born of
meditation, self-scrutiny, and a genuine delight in the
comparison of words and thoughts,—which were compared and contrasted, not for any ulterior purpose, but
solely for the scientific pleasure derived from accurate
classification and self-discipline.

Dr. Hawkins also taught Newman " the doctrine of
tradition," namely, that the tradition of the Church
was the original authority for doctrinal statements, and
that Scripture was never intended to supply the first
converts with their doctrinal creed, but only to afford
the verification of that creed with which the tradition of
the Church had furnished them. Just in the same way
no one would look in the law-reports for the systematic
doctrines of English law, or in parliamentary debates
for the accepted principles of the English constitution ;
but when the principles of English law and of the
English constitution had been explicitly laid down, the
authorities which laid them down would verify them
by references respectively to the law reports or
parliamentary debates.

Thus Newman early came to assume that the living
Church was the body to which we must still cling, both
for the explicit statement of our creed and for the explicit exposition of rites and their significance ; while
he regarded Scripture only as containing that body of
facts to which the Church referred as her authority for
the creed which she inculcated, and for the worship she
enjoined.

In his book on *The Arians of the Fourth Century*
Newman gave full expression to his confidence that
dogma is the backbone of religion, and this he has
always asserted with the utmost consistency and energy.
"From the age of fifteen," he says in the *Apologia*,
"dogma has been the fundamental principle of my
religion; I know no other religion; I cannot enter into
the idea of any other sort of religion; religion as a mere
sentiment is to me a dream and a mockery. As well
can there be filial love without the fact of a father, as
devotion without the fact of a Supreme Being. What
I held in 1816 I held in 1833, and I hold in 1864.
Please God I shall hold it to the end. Even when I
was under Dr. Whately's influence I had no temptation
to be less zealous for the great dogmas of the faith, and
at various times I used to resist such trains of thought
on his part as seemed to me (rightly or wrongly) to
obscure them."[1] I suppose that all clear-headed men
will agree with Cardinal Newman in admitting that,
without the confession of certain intellectual truths,
and without a careful sifting of what these truths are,
there is no possibility of the safe preservation of any
Divine revelation. But surely in this and other similar
passages of his works he a little confuses between the
intellectual conceptions which are necessarily implied
in the fact of revelation, and the life and character
which are the subjects of revelation. It is perfectly true
that we cannot have filial feelings without a father or
mother, and that we cannot have a father or mother
without a full intellectual assent to the assertion of
their existence, and to a good many other statements

[1] *Apologia*, p. 120.

as to the mind and character of that father or mother. But it is also perfectly true that many of those statements will be more or less mistaken,—deflected from the truth by our natural incapacity to enter fully into the mind and character of others. And therefore it does not in the least follow that, though there can be no true worship without our admitting the existence of God, and various great truths about God, all that we say about God need be nearly as certain as the very fact of His existence must be, nor even that all that is revealed about God need be quite as clear and quite as free from liability to misunder-standing as the great fact itself of His existence and of His holiness. If the great object of Christ's incarnation was the revelation of God Himself to the world, not the revelation of dogmas concerning God, then the primary object of Christ's life, and of the life of the Church, was the unveiling of the reality, for which purpose the due definition and guarding of dogma was only a secondary and subordinate duty. As the Church itself admitted, and even maintained, it was quite possible both to feel rightly and to think rightly in relation to God without using the best or most accurate words to express those right thoughts and right feelings; and again, it is perfectly easy to conceive that a multitude of Christians may have had the right feelings towards God without having had the most accurate and clearly defined thoughts concern-ing His essential being. Dogma is essential in order to display and safeguard the revelation, but dogma is not itself the revelation. And it is conceivable that in drawing out and safeguarding the revelation, the Church may not unfrequently have laid even too much

stress on right conceptions, and too little on right
attitudes of will and emotion. Dogma is only subsidiary
to that unveiling of God to man which is the single
aim of revelation, and instead of being made subsidiary,
it is sometimes made to stand in the place of that to
which it ought to be purely instrumental.

In his first theological book, that on *The Arians of the
Fourth Century*, Newman himself admitted this when he
said, " while the line of tradition, drawn out, as it was, to
the distance of two centuries from the Apostles, had at
length been of too frail a texture to resist the touch of
subtle and ill-directed reason, the Church was naturally
unwilling to have recourse to that novel though
necessary measure of imposing an authoritative creed
on those whom it invested with the office of teaching.
If I avow my belief that freedom from symbols and
articles is abstractedly the highest state of Christian
communion, and the peculiar privilege of the primitive
Church, it is not from any tenderness towards that
proud impatience of control in which many exult as in
a virtue, but first because technicality and formalism
are, in their degree, inevitable results of public confessions of faith; and next because, where confessions
do not exist, the mysteries of Divine truth, instead of
being exposed to the gaze of the profane and unin-
structed, are kept hidden in the bosom of the Church
far more faithfully than is otherwise possible, and
reserved, by a private teaching through the channel
of her ministers, as rewards in due measure and season
for those who are prepared to profit by them—for
those, that is, who are diligently passing through the
successive stages of faith and obedience." [1]

[1] *Arians of the Fourth Century*, chap. i. sec. ii.

The admission that "technicality and formalism" necessarily follow on dogmatic definitions is important, but hardly adequate to the truth. The real danger is, that the pains taken to understand, and avail themselves of, theological safeguards against error, shall supersede in men's minds the habit of gazing steadily at the fulness of the Divine character as gradually unveiled to them, though the diffusion of this habit is the end and aim of Hebrew prophecy and the purpose of Christ's life and death and resurrection. Dogma is analysis and inference, and necessarily inadequate analysis and inference. Such analysis and inference are forced on the Church by denials which tend to obscure the revelation given. But for those who were not likely to have been tempted and misled by those denials, dogmatic teaching may be positively mischievous as fixing their attention too exclusively on those aspects of revelation which are the least likely to develop a spiritual life. In *The Arians of the Fourth Century* Newman illustrated very effectively what he found in dogma that was really essential to the true apprehension of revelation.

And I cannot better deal with this early and very careful bit of work than by giving some specimen of its bearing on Newman's great principle that dogma is of the very essence of revelation. The book was finished in July, 1832, before the movement of 1833 began, and was published at the end of 1833. It may be said to have closed the first section of Newman's life. It is in many respects of high interest for its close reasoning and strict fidelity to principle, though it displays little of the literary skill of his later writings, being, indeed, dry almost to grittiness. If God, he says, did not send

His own Son into the world to be a ransom for sinners, and to inspire them with a new passion of devotion to their Creator, and a new loathing for the evil in themselves, then the whole story of revelation, of which the climax is anticipated in the account of Abraham's willingness to give up his only son Isaac at the invitation of God, is a dream, and the life of men on earth is robbed of its spiritual mainstay. Yet, in order to safeguard the truth of this revelation, if once it be denied and dissected by the sceptic, how much dogmatic analysis and definition, and of precautionary explanation is necessary! In fact, the whole Arian and Nestorian controversies are raised at once, so soon as an objector begins to recount the difficulties which beset the mind when it encounters such a revelation as this. If Christ were separate from God, then the love of God in giving up Christ to death for man would be in no wise specially attested; the sacrifice of Isaac would have been, in fact, a greater sacrifice, relatively to the power and character of the human being who made it, than was the sacrifice on Calvary. But if Christ were God, how much has to be explained in order to save this teaching from the alternative objection of either publishing to the world the love of a God who could cease to exist, or publishing something like a dramatic fiction in place of the greatest and most mysterious of all truths. Scripture insists, remarks Newman, that Christ is not only spoken of as God's Son in respect of His pre-existent nature, but in respect of His human nature, and that, in order to fix this idea firmly in our minds, He is called not only the Son of God in the state in which He lived before He appeared on earth, but absolutely God's "Son," or "only-begotten" Son. And this is announced in terms which are intended to assert that whatever was in God was in the Son of God. "As the Father hath life in Himself, so hath He given to the Son to have life in Himself . . . . that all men should honour the Son even as they honour the Father;" but then the word "Son" implies subordination, and Christ Himself asserted "My Father is greater than I;" and there the Arian conception at once enters, and if the word "Son" be too much insisted on in the sense which it bears in our human relations, there will be a tendency either to regard the Son of God as a creature, and therefore, so far as He is worshipped, there will be a tendency to worship a creature as Creator; or else in denying the Son of God the true Divine nature, to withdraw from Him all worship properly so called, which the Arians and Unitarians, who have legitimately developed the Arian idea, actually have done. But against this degradation of Christ from the divinity so persistently asserted for Him in Scripture, the whole drift of the revelation protests. And in order to secure the idea of "Son" from the materialistic misconceptions so engrafted on it, the revelation of Christ as the Word, or Reason, or Wisdom of God is given us, "to denote His essential presence in the Father in as full a sense as the attribute of wisdom is essential to Him." And also to denote His mediation —that it is *through* Him that the Father speaks to men—this declaration that the Son is also the Word of God is subjoined, and guards us against the impression that He is as individually distinct from the Father as a human son from a human father; indeed, it compels us to think of Him as identified with the Father in some sense much closer than sonship in its human aspects would imply. But here again comes in the

danger, that in speaking of Christ as the Word or
Wisdom of God, the sense of a separate personality
would be obliterated, which would end in the notion that
the Father died upon the cross. To obviate this danger
Christ is spoken of as the Word of God in a separate
personality, as a permanently existing, real, and living
Word, not as the mere breath or voice of the Father.
All these definitions are requisite in order to protect
the notion that Christ was at once " of God " and " in
God," without both of which it would be impossible to
read His life and death at once truly and spiritually
and to give Him the love and worship which He
claims. I have been obliged to summarize, but this
close piece of reasoning will give an age which has
almost forgotten what the claims of theological dogma
are, some insight into Newman's vigorous and strenuous
work.

Of course I have no intention of following Newman
through the careful and scholarly book on the Arians.
My only object is to make it quite clear, that in defending dogma he was defending what is at once essential
to the very life and essence of the story of Christ's sacrifice for man in which Divine revelation culminates,
and yet that in thus defending it, there is very great
danger of losing sight of the core of the revelation, and
indeed a moral certainty that many of those who would
never have killed the soul of revelation by insisting on
analyzing and dissecting its meaning for themselves,
have been diverted from what is most moving and most
elevating in it by the necessity of studying definitions
and explanations for which they had no craving and
would never have asked. I think the book shows that
to some extent Newman underrated this unfortunate

effect of dogma on the most spiritual minds, and that
he thought of dogma a little too much as the essence,
instead of as the mere protective covering, of revelation.
The substance of revelation is the character of God, and
dogma is only necessary to those whose minds cannot
enter into this marvellous revelation of the character
of God and of His love for man without asking a
hundred questions to which, in our present state, only
very imperfect and unsatisfactory answers can be given
—answers that only show how much greater are the
difficulties of the semi-sceptics than of the hearty believers, and do not show that Christian faith is itself
free from serious difficulty. In fact, the only attitude in
which the mere intellect of man can rest easily, is the
attitude of ignoring the whole difficulty and acquiescing
in pure agnosticism. But then that is an attitude in
which the soul of man cannot rest at all,—nor even the
intellect of a man who has a soul as well as an intellect. But for the predominantly intellectual, dogmatic
theology is a noble study, especially if it is so pursued
as to remind them that the most it can effect is to
point out the path of least resistance for the understanding that is coupled with a Christian heart and soul,
and the much greater difficulties into which the understanding must plunge if it passes into a heretical region
of thought. Theology, no doubt, is to some extent
truly described as a line of escape which passes between
the devil and the deep sea. If we are to believe with
all our hearts the only life-giving story of the Creator's
purposes and love, of which human history has furnished
us with any trace, we must take our way between
moral recklessness and self-will on the one side, and
that apathy which springs out of utter despair of finding

a solution for the problem of life on the other side. And no doubt even that way is not without its perils, but these perils can, I think, be shown to be much less than those of believers who, while clinging to the gospel of Christ, try to get rid of all the subtleties and distinctions of theological science. And this is what Newman's book on the Arians so carefully and elaborately shows.

The book, too, has another interest besides the great precision and delicacy with which Newman traced out the precise positions of the various heretical thinkers, from Sabellius to Arius, including the whole school of semi-Arians, who were the antagonists of Athanasius. It shows Newman's delight in the Alexandrian school of theology, with its emphatic teaching as to the secondary or allegorical interpretation of Scripture, its reserve and its very gradual unfolding of the mysteries of Christianity to its catechumens, its conception of the Divine "economy" of revelation, and its doctrine that fragments of the teaching that had been carefully concentrated and kept continuous for the benefit of the Jews, are to be found scattered widely through the Pagan world. Newman was the first to deny that Arianism was of Alexandrian origin, and to maintain, what scholars now generally admit, that it originated in Antioch. Indeed, Newman loved the Greek theology so well that he quickly discovered its essential orthodoxy, and the Judaizing affinities of the Arian heresy, which had previously been supposed to originate with Arius himself. Newman's book was meant as a vindication of the Alexandrian school of theology from all direct responsibility for that heresy. And in this I believe he fully succeeded.

As a great deal of the prejudice against Dr. Newman has been founded on his defence of the Alexandrian principle of spiritual economies to be practised
by men in teaching revealed truth, just as it was
practised by God in revealing it, I must say a few
words on that subject.   Newman pleads that St. Paul
was practising an "economy" when on Mars hill he
availed himself first of the altar erected to the Unknown
God, and next of the authority of a Greek for the
doctrine of God's fatherhood, instead of starting from
the ground of the Hebrew Scriptures, which was of
course his own starting-point; nay, that the first chapter
of the book of Job, in which Satan is represented as
commissioned by God to tempt Job and prove his
fidelity, and the twenty-second chapter of the first
book of Kings, in which God is represented as asking
for a lying spirit to entice Ahab to his destruction by
inducing the prophets of Israel to prophesy falsely concerning his engagement with the king of Syria at
Ramoth-gilead, are both evidently "economical" in the
sense that they do not convey absolute truth concerning
the ways of God, but only "substantial truth in the
form in which we were best able to receive it."   Again,
he argues that the Mosaic dispensation as a whole is
an obvious "economy" "simulating unchangeableness,
though from the first it was destined to be abolished."
In any case, our Lord's own declaration, "I have yet
many other things to say unto you, but ye cannot bear
them now.   Howbeit, when He, the Spirit of Truth,
is come, He shall guide you into all truth, for He
shall not speak of Himself; but whatsoever things He
shall hear, those shall He speak; and He shall show
you things to come," is as express a sanction of

" economy " as belonging to the very principle of God's revelation as can well be conceived; and it seems almost trivial to say that that which the providence of God sanctions, the prudence of man should not despise. Of course it is quite another question whether the conceit of prudence may not suggest, and sometimes practise, a mischievous reticence, and keep back portions of the Divine revelation which, if not withheld, would be the best fitted to make a profound impression on the heart. That is a question of individual judgment and moral insight; but to contend that the principle of economy is to be condemned *in toto*, is about as silly as to contend that what is suitable for impressing the hearts of grown-up men and women, is equally suitable for impressing the hearts of children; or that what is fitted for the ears of the highly-educated, is equally fitted for the ears of the ignorant and superstitious. I do not myself think that Newman can be justly accused of any disposition to push the principle of " economy " to excess. If he has ever done so, it is only by making occasional alterations in the original text of his own books without calling attention to them. And this has, I think, been rather due to a dislike for avowing the variations in his own judgment than to any dislike for speaking his mind freely enough while he is about it. The principle of " economy " is nothing in the world but good sense applied to the question of the best mode of bringing home God's truth to the minds of others.

D

CHAPTER III.

HURRELL FROUDE AND THE MEDITERRANEAN VOYAGE.

THE friendship between Newman and Mr. Hurrell
Froude, the elder brother of the historian, which commenced in 1826, and became intimate in 1829, lasting
thence to Mr. Froude's death from consumption in
1836, was certainly one of the most important influences
which acted on Newman's career at the most critical
period of his life. Newman's was one of the minds
which matured slowly, and it was not till he was
twenty-six years of age that it became clear whether he
would be in the main a religious leader or one of the
pillars of the Whately party, that is, the party who
threw their influence into the scale of minimizing the
spiritual aspect and spiritual significance of revelation
rather than of maximizing it. Newman himself mentions,
that for two or three years before 1827 he was "beginning to prefer intellectual excellence to moral," or in
other words, "drifting in the direction of Liberalism."
"I was rudely awakened from my dream at the end of
1827 by two great blows, illness and bereavement," and
then in 1829 came fuller intimacy with Hurrell Froude,
which seems to have fully determined, if anything were

then needed to determine, the direction in which his mind would proceed. Mr. Hurrell Froude was, as Newman describes him, a man of the highest gifts—gentle, tender, playful, versatile, and of the most winning patience and considerateness in discussion. He was a man of high genius, " brimful and overflowing with ideas and views, in him original, which were too many and strong even for his bodily strength, and which crowded and jostled against each other in their effort after distinct shape and expression. And he had an intellect as critical and logical as it was speculative and bold. He professed openly his admiration of the Church of Rome and his hatred of the Reformers. He delighted in the notion of an hierarchical system, of sacerdotal power, and of full ecclesiastical liberty. He felt scorn of the maxim ' the Bible and the Bible only as the religion of Protestants ' ; and he gloried in accepting tradition as a main instrument of religious teaching. He had a high, severe idea of the intrinsic excellence of virginity, and he considered the Blessed Virgin the great pattern. He delighted in thinking of the saints; he had a keen appreciation of the idea of sanctity, its possibility and its heights, and he was more than inclined to believe a large amount of miraculous interference as occurring in the early and middle ages. He embraced the principle of penance and mortification. He had a deep devotion to the Real Presence, in which he had a firm faith. He was powerfully drawn to the mediæval Church, but not to the primitive." Dr. Newman adds, that Hurrell Froude "was fond of historical inquiry and the politics of religion. He had no turn for theology as such. He had no appreciation of the writings of the Fathers, of the detail or development of doctrine, of the definite traditions of the Church viewed in their matter, of the teaching of the Œcumenical Councils, or of the controversies out of which they arose." He was "a high Tory of the Cavalier stamp, and was disgusted with the Toryism of the opponents of the Reform Bill." [1] And I feel little doubt that Dr. Newman's wrath against "Liberalism," as for many years afterwards he always called it,—identifying as he did Liberalism with Latitudinarianism,—was to a very considerable extent a moral contagion caught from Hurrell Froude.

There are a few singularly beautiful lines added by Newman after Hurrell Froude's death in 1836 to the exquisite poem called *Separation of Friends*, written in 1833; and these sufficiently prove the tenderness of Newman's friendship for Hurrell Froude, and the intimacy of the relation between them. The poem as it was first written on the separation between friends caused by death, ran thus—

> " Do not their souls, who 'neath the altar wait
>   Until their second birth,
> The gift of patience need, as separate
>   From their first friends of earth ?
> Not that earth's blessings are not all outshone
>   By Eden's Angel flame,
> But that Earth knows not that the Dead has won
>   That Crown which was his aim.
> For when he left it, 'twas a twilight scene
>   About his silent bier,
> A breathless struggle, Faith and Sight between,
>   And Hope and sacred Fear.
> Fear startled at his pains and dreary end,
>   Hope raised her chalice high,
> And the twin-sisters still his shade attend,
>   Viewed in the mourner's eye.

[1] *Apologia*, pp. 84-6.

So day by day for him from earth ascends,
    As dew in summer even,
The speechless intercession of his friends,
    Towards the azure heaven."

This was an abrupt close. Nearly three years later
it appeared that the true close had but been reserved
till the friend with whom in his illness Newman had
been travelling, had left him alone here to offer this
"speechless intercession" on behalf of him who had
departed. Then after Froude's death, on the 28th
February, 1836, Newman added the final lines—

"Ah ! dearest, with a word he could dispel
    All questioning, and raise
Our hearts to rapture, whispering all was well,
    And turning prayer to praise.
And other secrets too he could declare,
    By patterns all divine,
His earthly creed retouching here and there,
    And deepening every line.
Dearest ! he longs to speak as I to know,
    And yet we both refrain :
It were not good ; a little doubt below,
    And all will soon be plain."

Such was Newman's feeling for the friend—already
suffering from the commencement of the consumption
of which he died three years later—with whom he
visited the Mediterranean, between December 1832 and
April 1833, when they separated at Rome—Newman to
turn to Sicily, where he fell ill, and to spend something like three months of solitude after his four months'
voyage along the African, Greek, and Italian coasts. It
was on this journey that the remarkable series of verses
afterwards published with the signature δ in the *Lyra
Apostolica,*—some of them poems of the purest beauty,

some of them mere doctrinal or didactic or theologico-political anathemas,—were first written.

The isles of Greece are closely associated with another great name, but it would be hard to find a more marvellous contrast than that between the attitude of feeling with which Byron gazed on the scenes in which "burning Sappho lived and sung," and where, as, with his genuine passion for political liberty, he delighted to remember, there "grew the arts of war and peace," and that with which Newman and Froude, well versed indeed in the classical associations of those rocky shores, but still more deeply interested in the ecclesiastical memories they stirred, gazed upon them. They visited Ithaca, but in his poems written "off Ithaca" Newman never mentions the name of Ulysses, though in passing Lisbon he had recalled that strong pagan figure in the lines which he headed *The Isles of the Sirens*—

> " Cease, stranger, cease those piercing notes,
>   The craft of Siren choirs ;
> Hush the seductive voice that floats
>   Upon the languid wires.
>
> Music's ethereal fire was given,
>   Not to dissolve our clay,
> But draw Promethean beams from Heaven,
>   And purge the dross away.
>
> Weak self ! with thee the mischief lies—
>   Those throbs a tale disclose ;
> Nor age nor trial has made wise
>   The Man of many woes."

There you see some trace of the influence of Froude's high ascetic nature speaking in the heart of a devotee of music, but a devotee of music of the most exalted kind. Hurrell Froude in a letter home mentions that the commander of the steamer in which they

sailed sang several songs, accompanying himself on the
Spanish guitar, and it must have been these songs which
suggested to Newman *The Isles of the Sirens.*

When the friends reach Ithaca, Newman seems to
forget " the man of many woes " altogether ; he is musing
on the difficulty and duty of keeping himself " unspotted
from the world," which is the last thing I suppose
that Homer's Ulysses ever thought about, while Byron
in the same scenes thought only of how he could spot
himself most effectually ; or if Newman indulges for
a moment in the reminiscence of that strong ideal
passion for his native country which made Ulysses pine
for the bare and rocky islet amidst the seductions of
the isle of Calypso and the flattery of his Phæacian
hosts, it only suggests to him to paint that ideal
patriotism which inspired the longing of Moses to tread
the soil of Canaan in the hour of his death upon Mount
Nebo, and which has so often served the Christian in
place of patriotism when contemplating a home for
which his soul had yearned, but the soil of which he
has never trodden.

THE DEATH OF MOSES.

" My Fathers' hope ! my childhood's dream !
     The promise from on high !
Long waited for ! its glories beam
     Now when my death is nigh.

My death is come, but not decay ;
     Nor eye nor mind is dim ;
The keenness of youth's vigorous day
     Thrills in each nerve and limb.

Blest scene ! thrice welcome after toil—
     If no deceit I view ;
O might my lips but press the soil
     And prove the vision true !

> Its glorious heights, its wealthy plains,
>   Its many-tinted groves,
> They call ! but He my steps restrains
>   Who chastens whom He loves.
>
> Ah ! now they melt . . . they are but shades . .
>   I die !—yet is no rest,
> O Lord ! in store, since Canaan fades,
>   But seen, and not possest ! "

That was written " off Ithaca," on the 30th December,
1832. Newman's nostalgia was more in sympathy with
that of Moses than with that of Ulysses; the home he
longed for was a home he had never yet gained. There is
something very strange in the connection between these
classical scenes and the thoughts they excited in the
travellers, for I cannot help thinking that most of these
poems must have owed their origin almost as much to
Froude's suggestion as to Newman's pen. The lines, for
instance, on "England," in which Newman calls her "Tyre
of the West," and accuses her of trusting in such poor
defences as the fortified rock of Gibraltar, and such
poor resources as her rich commerce supplied, look as
if they had owed a good deal of their inspiration to
Froude's cavalier contempt for the wealth earned by
trade, as well as his scorn for any ostentatious display
of power not rooted in a devout theocratic faith. Off
Zante Newman muses on "the Greek fathers," and
passes by " the heathen praise " of Greece, to recall the
Christian achievements of Clement, Dionysius, Origen,
and Basil, Gregory of Nazianzen, and "royal-hearted
Athanase, with Paul's own mantle blest." At Corcyra
he cannot forget his Thucydides, it is true, but the turn
he gives to the reflections the historian had suggested
to him directed his thoughts again to the political
ruthlessness of maritime power, and the individual

responsibility of each member of a nation for his share
in its fierce and cruel deeds.

> " I sat beneath an olive's branches gray,
>   And gazed upon the site of a lost town,
>   By sage and poet chosen for renown ;
> There dwelt a race that on the sea held sway,
> And, restless as its waters, forced a way
>   For civil strife a thousand states to drown.
> That multitudinous stream we now note down,
>   As though one life, in birth and in decay.
> Yet, is their being's history spent and run,
>   Whose spirits live in awful singleness,
> Each in his self-formed sphere of light or gloom ?
> Henceforth, while pondering the fierce deeds then done,
> Such reverence on me shall its seal impress,
>   As though I corpses saw, and walked the tomb."

There is to me something very striking in the
contrast between the class of thoughts which the old
Greek and Roman localities suggest to a Whig poet like
Byron, with a broad dash of license in his whiggery, to
classical scholars like Clough, imbued with what is now
called " the modern spirit,"—as well its moral earnestness as its intellectual scepticism,—and to grave spirits
like Newman's and Hurrell Froude's, dominated not only
by a religious but by a strongly-marked ecclesiastical bias.
Hurrell Froude writes from Rome—" Rome is the place,
after all, where there is most to astonish one, and of all
ages, even the present. I don't know that I take much
interest in the relics of the empire, magnificent as
they are, although there is something sentimental in
seeing (as one literally may) the cows and oxen, ' Roman-
oque foro et lautis mugire carinis.'   But the thing
which most takes possession of one's mind is the entire
absorption of the old Roman splendour in an unthought-
of system ; to see their columns, the marbles and bronzes

which had been brought together at such an immense
cost, all diverted from their first objects, and taken up
by Christianity—St. Peter and St. Paul standing at the
top of Trajan's and Antonine's columns, and St. Peter
buried in the Circus of Nero, with all the splendour of
Rome concentrated in his mausoleum."[1]   The effect
of all this on Newman, who at this time had not yet got
over his strong prepossession against the Church of
Rome, was rather to repel him and drive him into
dwelling on the simplicity and modesty of the primitive
Church, than to pre-engage his imagination for the faith
to which he ultimately resigned himself.   At Messina,
for instance, he complains of the fascination exerted
over his heart by "these scenes of ancient heathen
fame," and by the associations which the poetry of Virgil
and Horace had made so dear to him, and reproaches
himself that the "shades of power and those who bore a
part in the mad deeds that set the world in flame,"
should still charm his imagination, excusing himself
on the old plea "homo sum ; nihil humani a me alienum
puto;" and as a rule the more striking the associations of
the place, the more he retreats into reveries on the
Divine warnings which rebuke earthly pride, and on
that call to renounce their fondest dreams by which the
heroes of God's grace have been distinguished.   Just
as before he started on his tour he had impressed upon
himself, at Hurrell Froude's Devonshire home, Darting-
ton, that he must never indulge the enthusiasm he was
capable of feeling for "streamlet bright, and soft
secluded grove," since he had vowed himself to higher
affections ; so in the great scenes of classical antiquity

---

[1] Froude's *Remains*, vol. i. pp. 298, 299.

he schooled himself to draw back with so much the
sterner resolution from the natural associations of the
place, to those Divine lessons which Scripture contained.
Two of his finest poems on David were written in quaran-
tine at Malta. At Frascati he reproaches himself for
feeling so keenly the temptations of the world around
him, and hopes for the time when he shall no longer
"feel a secret joy that hell is near." At Tre Fontani he
thanks God that he has been drawn on so gradually to
the conviction that he must lead a lonely life devoted to
his missionary work; and it is only at Palermo, after
his serious illness in Sicily, and while waiting impa-
tiently for the means of returning home, that he allows
himself to take some comfort in visiting the Roman
Catholic Churches, and accepting their soothing influence, as the gifts of a good Samaritan to a wounded
wanderer. He exclaims—

" O that thy creed were sound !
    For thou dost soothe the heart, thou Church of Rome,
By thy unwearied watch and varied round
    Of service, in thy Saviour's holy home.
I cannot walk the city's sultry streets,
But the wide porch invites to still retreats,
    Where passion's thirst is calmed, and care's unthankful gloom.

There, on a foreign shore,
    The homesick solitary finds a friend :
Thoughts, prisoned long for lack of speech, outpour
    Their tears ; and doubts in resignation end.
I almost fainted from the long delay,
That tangles me within this languid bay,
    When comes a foe, my wounds with oil and wine to tend."

So that the Church of Rome, though doing for him
the office of the good Samaritan, is still to him "a foe."
It is when he is fairly on his voyage back to under-
take that work which throughout his dangerous illness

he was so deeply convinced that he had yet to do in
England, as to fill him with the assurance that he should
not die, that his most exquisite poems were written,
—those verses shining with the softest and the whitest
poetic lustre, which have fairly conquered even the
admiration of the severest Protestant Churches, addressed to the "kindly light" which he entreated,
"amidst the encircling gloom," to lead him on; and
the two splendid studies in the style of the tragic Greek
chorus, one of which I have given at length in a previous chapter. For grandeur of outline, purity of taste,
and radiance of total effect, I know hardly any short
poems in the language that equal them.

As regards the influence of this journey on Newman's
future career, it appears that while in many respects
it diminished his horror of Romanism, in consequence
especially of the influence of Hurrell Froude, it had
a contrary effect on Hurrell Froude's own mind, and
later again, through him to some extent I suppose,
on Newman's. Hurrell Froude writes from Naples on
the 17th February, 1833—"I remember you told me
that I should come back a better Englishman than
I went away; better satisfied not only that our
Church is nearest in theory right, but also that practically, in spite of its abuses, it works better; and
to own the truth, your prophecy is already nearly
realized. Certainly I have as yet only seen the surface of things, but what I have seen does not come
up to my notions of propriety. These Catholic countries
seem in an especial manner κατέχειν τὴν ἀλήθειαν ἐν
ἀδικίᾳ, and the priesthood are themselves so sensible
of the hollow basis on which their power rests, that they
dare not resist the most atrocious encroachments of the

State upon their privileges."[1] And after detailing the
abuses of the Roman Catholic system in Sicily he goes
on, "The Church of England has fallen low, and will
probably be worse before it is better; but let the Whigs
do their worst, they cannot sink us so deep as these
people have allowed themselves to fall, while retaining
all the superficials of a religious country."[2] When it
is considered that this was the impression of Roman
Catholicism, judged by its fruits, which that one of the
two friends who was by far the most inclined to the
Roman system brought away from his life in a Roman
Catholic country, we cannot wonder that Newman
should have remained for eight more years a zealous
Anglican, before he even began to foresee clearly
whither he was tending.

[1] Hurrell Froude's *Remains*, vol. i. p. 293.
[2] *Ibid.* p. 294.

CHAPTER IV.

NEWMAN'S RELATION TO THE TRACTARIAN MOVEMENT.

DURING the whole of his Mediterranean journey
Newman was, as we have seen, profoundly impressed
with the conviction that he and the band of friends
who wished to restore the authority of the Church of
England had a great work before them. In Rome
Newman and Froude had an interview with Monseigneur,
afterwards Cardinal, Wiseman, and the latter expressed
a wish in parting that they might make a second visit to
Rome, to which Newman replied "with great gravity,
'We have a work to do in England.'" He adds, "I
went down at once to Sicily, and the presentiment grew
stronger. I struck into the middle of the island, and
fell ill of a fever at Leonforte. My servant thought
that I should die, and begged for my last directions.
I gave them as he wished, but I said, 'I shall not die.'
I repeated, 'I shall not die, for I have not sinned
against light, I have not sinned against light.' I have
never been able," he adds in the *Apologia*, "to make
out at all what I meant. I got to Castra Giovanni, and
was laid up there for nearly three weeks. Towards
the end of May I set off for Palermo, taking three days
for the journey. Before starting from my inn on the

morning of May 26th or 27th, I sat down on my bed
and began to sob bitterly. My servant, who had acted
as my nurse, asked what ailed me. I could only answer,
'I have a work to do in England.'" On the Sunday after
his arrival at home, namely, July 14th, 1833, Mr. Keble
preached the Assize sermon in the University pulpit.
"It was published," says Newman, "under the title of
National Apostasy. I have ever considered and kept
the day as the start of the religious movement of 1833."
It was the forty-fourth anniversary of the taking of
the Bastille, which the French people keep as the
anniversary of the great Revolution. The Tractarian
movement was no doubt in its tendency distinctly
anti-revolutionary, for it not only used "Liberalism"
as the name for its chief foe, identifying, as it then
did, Liberalism with Latitudinarianism, but it proved a
distinctly clerical movement, while the Revolutionary
party in France has always regarded "clericalism" as a
foe even more bitter than the Church of Rome herself.
Now Tractarianism was clerical to the core—more
clerical, I conceive, in some real sense than the Roman
Catholic Church herself. The recoil against the world
which made Newman so unwilling to recall even the
glories of pagan antiquity when he was abroad, the
semi-evangelical, semi-ascetic dread of any but a *consciously* religious life, which marked the poems and
tendencies of 1833, all seemed to imply a somewhat
rigid form of sacerdotalism. In the very first of the
Tracts for the Times which was written by Newman
himself he asks, "On what are we to rest our authority
when the State deserts us?" and the answer given is,
"On our Apostolical descent." Of course the Roman
Catholic Church would give the same answer, but there

is a great difference between the attitude of a Church which has always and notoriously rested on the claim of Apostolic descent, and a Church which puts in such a claim at a time when a very considerable proportion of its clergy repudiate it, and when the claim sounds to the ears of most men strange and paradoxical. This was so much the case in the Anglican Church that Newman tells a story of one of the bishops, " who on reading an early *Tract on the Apostolical Succession* could not make up his mind whether he held the doctrine or not." But of course in such a condition of things the claim for the Apostolical succession forced the party which made it into a much more pronounced and self-conscious, not to say almost aggressive and even pretentious, type of sacerdotalism than that of a Church wherein direct Apostolical succession had been the plainly and universally avowed basis of the priesthood for nearly two thousand years. And Newman's personal attitude gave a great deal of additional effect to the ostentatiously sacerdotal tone of the party. " I thought," he says, " that the Apostolical form of doctrine was essential and imperative, and its grounds of evidence impregnable. Owing to this confidence, it came to pass at that time that there was a double aspect in my bearing towards others, which it is necessary for me to enlarge on. My behaviour had a mixture in it both of fierceness and of sport, and on this account, I dare say, it gave offence to many; nor am I here defending it." [1] " I was not unwilling to draw an opponent on step by step to the brink of some intellectual absurdity, and to leave him to get back

[1] *Apologia*, p. 114.

as he could. I was not unwilling to play with a man who asked impertinent questions. I think I had in my mouth the words of the wise man, 'Answer a fool according to his folly,' especially if he was prying or spiteful. I was reckless of the gossip which was circulated about me, and when I might easily have set it right, did not deign to do so. Also I used irony in conversation, when matter-of-fact men could not see what I meant."[1] And then what Newman calls his occasional "fierceness" was equally well calculated to impress men with his setting up a new order of things on a definitely sacerdotal basis. "In the very first page of the first Tract," he tells us, "I said of the bishops that, 'black event though it would be for the country, yet we could not wish them a more blessed termination of their course than the spoiling of their goods and martyrdom.'"[2] "Again, when one of my friends of liberal and evangelical opinions wrote to expostulate with me on the course I was taking, I said that we would ride over him and his as Othniel prevailed over Chushan Rishathaim, King of Mesopotamia. Again, I would have no dealings with my brother, and I put my conduct upon a syllogism. I said, 'St. Paul bids us avoid those who cause divisions; you cause divisions, therefore I must avoid you.' I dissuaded a lady from attending the marriage of a sister who had seceded from the Anglican Church."[3]

All this gave an impression that the head of the movement which claimed Apostolical succession as the foundation of the order of the Anglican Church was himself almost "fiercely" sacerdotal. I don't think

---

[1] *Apologia*, p. 115.   [2] *Ibid.* p. 117.   [3] *Ibid.* p. 118.

that that ever was his character at all. Indeed, I think his was very much the reverse of a specially sacerdotal character. Cardinal Newman has always been too shy and too reserved a man, with too individual a nature, to care to assert effectively for a caste the sway it should theoretically exert over his fellow-men. Least of all would he care to exercise that sway through the respect felt for his position as a priest, rather than through the affection felt for his person as an individual. But it is perfectly true, I think, that he regarded an authoritative Church as at least as important an element in revelation as a clearly-defined doctrine, and that, so far as I can judge, he never gave that pre-eminence to the gradual unveiling of the character of God as the main subject-matter of revelation, which could alone, I suppose, hold sufficiently in check the tendency to exalt and magnify the function of the priesthood.

Newman was always more or less disposed to accept Bishop Butler's principle, that probability is the guide of life (though, as I have shown, he did not think it could be applied to enforce the duty of prayer on those who only believed the existence of God to be a highly probable hypothesis), to a much greater extent than I should have thought either safe or in conformity with our Lord's teaching, and hence he attached a much greater relative importance to the institutions which grew up under the Gospel as significant parts of the Divine purpose of revelation, than they were perhaps intended to bear. He thought as much, I suppose, of the effect—in the direction of humility, for example—which the habit of confession and the ordinance of absolution would produce on the human character, as he thought of the effect in the same direction which the constant study of Christ's character would produce, for him and his colleagues. Revelation meant not merely, perhaps not chiefly, the unveiling of the Divine character and personality, but the totality of the results to be produced by all the new agencies which Christianity set in motion, and of these of course he regarded an authoritative Church as by far the most important. To him the Church, instead of being merely the great organization which handed down to future generations the original testimony to Christ, and which strove to embody His teaching in actual practice, was in the first instance the depository of the sacraments which Christ instituted, and became through their instrumentality the only agency competent to impress adequately on the soul those regenerate habits of mind which could alone make that testimony effectual.

Newman and his friends hold, if I understand them rightly, that the institutions that grew up in the kingdom of God, which our Lord announced, counted for at least as much in relation to the salvation of men as the unveiling of God's character itself,—this kingdom of God being another name for the Church into which the Apostles (and their successors) were to have the power of admitting those who were willing to submit to the appropriate conditions. But this implied definite conditions under which alone valid sacraments could be granted and received, and a certain number of traditional principles by which the ministers of these sacraments must be bound. Questions relating to the Church generally became, therefore, in the minds of those who held that these sacraments were of the first importance as agents of spiritual life, not mere ecclesiastical questions, but questions of theology of the utmost significance, questions of theology at least as weighty as the due unveiling of the Divine character itself. Hurrell Froude, in the remarkable essay on *Rationalism as shown in the Interpretation of Scripture,* which seems to present the Tractarian view of the Church and its agency with singular clearness, maintains that Christ, in breathing on His Apostles, gave them the power of transmitting to others the gift which He had bestowed on them, by prayer and the laying on of hands; that the Apostles did so transmit it to others, and they again to others, and that in this way only it has been preserved in the world to the present day. This gift, it was contended, also bestows the power to admit into communion and to exclude from it; to bless and intercede for those who are in communion; to bless bread and wine so as to create the body and blood of Christ in the same sense in which our Lord's blessing made them so; and "to enable delegates to perform this great miracle by ordaining them with imposition of hands."

It was frankly admitted by the leading Tractarians,— and explicitly by both Newman and Froude,—that there is comparatively little explicit statement in the New Testament on the subject of these most important terms of communion and the privileges of communicants, and that it is somewhat mysterious that there is so little, though they held that what there is on the subject is very impressive, and quite sufficient to direct attention to the significance of the traditional teaching on this head. Of course they supplemented the evidence, which they regarded as so deficient in Scripture, by the teaching and practice of the primitive Church in the earliest age in which its teaching and practice are intimately known to us. And so far as the evidence still seemed more or less inadequate, they schooled themselves with Bishop Butler's doctrine, that the Almighty, in revealing to us any part of His will in writing, has done more than we had any reason to expect, and that consequently He may have left many parts of it unrevealed in writing, for aught reason tells us to the contrary. They argued, that so soon as we have clear evidence of the tendency of God's will from any one source, natural piety ought to make us eager to supplement our knowledge of it, so far as it is possible to do so from any other sufficient source of knowledge, just as a son who had certain documentary evidence of his father's wishes would, if he heartily loved that father, be eager to supplement the knowledge so acquired by the oral testimony of any credible witnesses of his father's death, who should tell him that he had expressed wishes to them about him which were not embodied in the formal will. And they argued, that if a generously filial spirit would show itself by accepting such credible oral testimony, then it is reasonable for Christians to supplement the teaching of the New Testament as to our Lord's purpose by the evidence of the friends and successors of the Apostles, as it was embodied in the habits and devotions of the primitive Church. Especially they insisted that in the case supposed as to the father's will, the son would be doubly eager to guide himself by the oral evidence of those who were around the death-bed, if the drift of these unwritten directions tended on the whole to enforce on him self-denial and self-sacrifice, for this would increase the obligation on him for cir-cumspection, and abridge his right to do as he pleased with the property. And this was the case, they contended, as regarded the traditional practice of the primitive Church with regard to the use and conditions of the sacraments. And they pressed Butler's use of the doctrine that probability is the guide of life, most earnestly when it came to the question as to the *amount* of evidence. Even, they said, if we can only convince ourselves that there is a slight presumption that it was Christ's will that we should govern ourselves by the ordinances and practices of the primitive Church, we are as much bound to act upon that presumption,—supposing, of course, that there is nothing contrary in it to His known will,—as if we had the fullest proof that it was so. Indeed, they went further, and urged that probably the speculative difficulties in which the evidence of some parts of religion is involved, is a providential part of some persons' trial, and the only sort of trial which would really provide them with the proper materials for the discipline of their own character. Such people feel no temptation to the ordinary sins of injustice, unrestrained pleasure-seeking, and irreligion, but they need discipline for their wills just as much as those who are so tempted, and for them the true discipline is to act on a presumption as to what God's will is, which they know to be anything but certain, and that too with as much earnestness and dutifulness as they would act on it if they had the most final evidence that it is His will.

I insist upon this very marked element in the Tractarian movement, because it distinguished the whole genius of that movement. It gave the Tractarians the same anxious, and, as I may call it, precautionary piety which distinguished the great Bishop Butler's type of religion, and which is as different from the implicit and joyous confidence which the Roman Catholics place in their Church, as it is from the sober conventionalism of the religion of the "Establishment."

It will be seen later, that when Newman at last made up his mind to join the Church of Rome, his genius bloomed out with a force and freedom such as it never displayed in the Anglican communion, though he belonged to that communion till he was forty-four years of age. And I ascribe a good deal of its repression during the twelve years between 1833 and 1845 to that habit of schooling himself to act on assumptions of which there could be no certitude, which the Tractarian party, conscious that it was proposing a religious system more or less alien to the temper of their Church, forced itself to adopt. The Tractarians lived more like a colony of immigrants amongst a people of different language and customs, than like a band of patriots who were reviving the old glories of their native country. Indeed, they felt that they were acting on a hypothesis which was not only intrinsically doubtful, but as yet unacclimatized to the soil of English Churchmanship, and which did not take very kindly to that soil.

The following passage from Hurrell Froude's essay on *Rationalism as shown in the Interpretations of Scripture*, embodies very adequately the principles of the Tractarian movement. After admitting that the ancient belief of the Church respecting the sacraments and the priesthood "is not forced upon us by Scripture," and that "the texts which seem to imply it do not necessarily imply it," he goes on—"Hence it is inferred that they certainly do not imply it; that it is not alluded to in

Scripture; and is therefore a foolish if not criminal
superstition. Persons who think in this manner will do
well to recollect that there are in the Bible the following words,—'Thomas, because thou hast seen Me thou
hast believed; blessed are they that have not seen and
yet have believed.' These words do not apply directly
either to the sacred elements or to the priesthood;
primarily they refer to our Lord's resurrection, not to
the institutions which were the standing monuments
of it; yet they are not the words of one who would be
exceedingly displeased at our accepting even these on
evidence short of demonstration. 'Blessed are they
that have not seen and yet have believed'—this declaration (humanly speaking) is strangely unguarded, if a
generous, unsuspecting reverence for all that claims to
be from Him is indeed so dangerous a temper; nor do I
think that man's condition an unenviable one who at the
last day shall plead as validly for all his errors as this
text will plead for those of a ready faith. If at that
day it shall indeed prove true that sacerdotal Benedic-
tions and Absolutions, and the mysterious Consecration
of the Bread and Wine, are nothing more than many
a zealous Protestant would reduce them to; and the
reverence of those who have bowed to them as Christ's
ordinances, shall thus turn out to have been superfluous,
is it to be thought that the fear to reject what might
possibly be from the Lord, will prove no excuse for
having accepted what was not? that the temper which
has in these instances been led astray by trusting
evidence short of demonstration, will find no grace in
His eyes who reproved the incredulity of Thomas?"

Thus the very core of the Tractarian movement
was a precautionary creed for which the leaders felt

that the evidence was doubtful, but which they held to be more likely than not, and in any case to be an ecclesiastical "working hypothesis" on which it was their duty to act. This attitude of mind it was that tinged the whole Tractarian movement with an air of anxious venturesomeness, of hesitating audacity, of care-worn courage, which was as foreign as possible to the spirit of the Anglican Church in which it originated, and as different as possible from the spirit of the Roman Catholic Church in which it found its goal. That Newman himself adopted this tone as explicitly as either Froude or any other of the leaders, is demon-strable. "If we will doubt," he wrote in Tract 85, "that is, if we will not allow evidence to be sufficient which merely results in a balance on the side of revelation; if we will determine that no evidence is enough to prove revealed doctrine but what is overpowering; if we will not go by evidence in which there are (so to say) three chances for revelation and only two against, we cannot be Christians; we shall miss Christ either in His inspired Scriptures, or in His doctrines, or in His ordinances." It is characteristic of the change in Newman's views, that in republishing this tract with all the necessary retractations after his conversion to the Roman Catholic Church, he did not allow this sentence to stand as it stands here, even though it was covered by the necessary retractations, and altered it into "*a dozen* chances for revelation and only two against," instead of "three chances for revelation and only two against." In other words, he evidently held that even as a Protestant he had underrated the magnitude of the probability on which he believed, and that he had actually felt a much larger confidence in the truth of his assumption than his language at the time expressed. And that was no doubt really the case. In his extreme anxiety not to understate the difficulties with which he was grappling, he often, I think, in his Tractarian days, gave an impression of a much more doubtful attitude of mind than he had really been conscious of.

And this leads me naturally to the charge which has so often been brought against him, that with a profoundly sceptical intellect, he forced upon himself a belief which was not only not the true conclusion of his unbiased mind, but was one which he had implicitly, though not perhaps with full consciousness, rejected. Let me add, however, that Newman's attitude in the movement was always far more hesitating, precautionary, and tentative than that of Ward and the advanced party. But Mr. Wilfrid Ward's admirable life of his father has given so powerful a sketch of the tone of the right wing of the Tractarian movement, that it is quite unnecessary for me to dwell upon it at any length.

CHAPTER V.

NEWMAN'S ALLEGED SCEPTICISM.

I QUOTED at the opening of this essay a passage in which Professor Huxley suggests that it would be easy to extract a very effective "Primer of Infidelity" from Cardinal Newman's writings, especially from the *Essay on Ecclesiastical Miracles,* the Tract 85 on *Holy Scripture in Relation to the Catholic Creed,* and the *Essay on Development.* And I admit that this might be accomplished; and yet I no more admit that Newman's mind is essentially sceptical, than I admit that Professor Huxley's is essentially credulous because it would be possible by careful selection to get a good deal out of his writings which might furnish a primer of fundamental beliefs. The very passage by which Professor Huxley illustrates his remark will serve admirably to show how very empty of true significance the remark is. He says that "there is something really impressive in the magnificent contempt with which Dr. Newman sweeps aside alike those who offer and those who demand what ordinary men call evidence for miracles." And in proof of this he quotes the following from the *Essay on Ecclesiastical Miracles*—

"Some infidel authors advise us to accept no miracles which would not have a verdict in their favour in a Court of Justice; that is, they employ against Scripture a

weapon which Protestants would confine to attacks
upon the Church; as if moral and religious questions
required legal proofs, and evidence were the test of
truth." [1] And Professor Huxley goes on—"'As if
evidence were the test of truth!' although the truth in
question is the occurrence or non-occurrence of certain
phenomena at a certain time or place. This sudden
revelation of the great gulf fixed between the ecclesiastical and the scientific mind, is enough to take away
the breath of one unfamiliar with the clerical organ."
I should rather say that this remark of Professor
Huxley's, as coming from one who professes familiarity
with the essay in question, is enough to take away
the breath of any one unfamiliar with the scientific
organ. Read in its context, Dr. Newman's observation
is not only not startling, but is a mere truism.
The essayist had been arguing that a fact may be,
and is in multitudes of instances, just as true even
though there be no evidence to prove it true, as it
is when it is attested by the most incontrovertible
evidence. The evidence may be our best or even our
only ground for believing it, but the absence of such
evidence does not in the least disprove the reality of
the fact, it only deprives us of any good reason for
believing the fact.

Professor Huxley would be about the last man,
I suppose, to maintain that evidence is really the
test of truth, instead of being merely the path by
which we obtain access to the truth. There are
millions of truths to which we have as yet no access
because we have no evidence of them, but which are

[1] *Two Essays on Scripture Miracles and on Ecclesiastical*, by
John Henry Newman. Second edition, p. 231.

nevertheless just as much truths as the ponderability of the atmosphere was a truth for all the centuries before it was discovered that the air had weight, or the tendency of the moon to fall towards the earth before Newton discovered it. Instead of revealing "the great gulf fixed between the ecclesiastical and the scientific mind," the words of Newman which Professor Huxley quotes are indefinitely more strict and scientific than the very unscientific words in which his scientific opponent criticizes them. Indeed, a greater or more careless bit of interpretation of a very exact writer I never read than Professor Huxley's criticism. Newman's whole drift in the passage from which Professor Huxley makes what he seems to consider this startling extract, is as plain as words can make it. He reminds his readers that evidence for a class of facts is of two kinds—the evidence that there is such a class of facts in existence, and the evidence that a particular event belonging to that class really took place. He insists that when evidence for the real existence of the class has been satisfactorily made out, the strong antecedent improbability against a totally new class of facts is removed, and that it is then reason-able to accept much less convincing evidence on the second head than we ought to require if we had reason to doubt whether such a class of facts existed at all. But even when we are satisfied on that head, he insists that in reference to events of this kind which excite men's wonder and admiration, we ought "to be pre-pared for fiction and exaggeration in the narrative to an indefinite extent." [1] He believes in all the Scripture

[1] *Two Essays on Scripture Miracles and on Ecclesiastical*, by John Henry Newman. Second edition, p. 229.

miracles, because he believes in "the inspiration of
Scripture" as imposed upon us by the same authority
which has given us revelation as a whole; but he points
out that, apart from the general principle of the inspiration of Scripture, there are very many of the Scripture
miracles in which there would be nothing in the
narrative to compel belief. Of course he maintains,
with all the apologists, that there are leading miracles,
like the resurrection of our Lord, which are supported
by an overwhelming amount of proof, at all events
to all those who begin with a belief in God, and an
expectation therefore of some manifestation to men
of His character and purposes. He holds with regard
to miracles, that only "a few can be exhibited with
evidence of so cogent and complete a character as to
demand his [the student's] acceptance," apart from the
general principle of the inspiration of Scripture, which
he regards as covering all Scripture miracles which would
otherwise be doubtful; while as to the alleged miracles
of ecclesiastical history, "a great number of them, as
far as the evidence goes, are neither entirely true nor
entirely false, but have very various degrees of probability viewed one with another; all of them recommended
to his [the student's] devout attention by the circum-
stance that others of the same family have been proved
to be true, and all prejudiced by his knowledge that
so many others, on the contrary, are certainly not true.
It will be his wisdom, then, not to reject or scorn
accounts of miracles where there is a fair chance of
their being true; but to allow himself to be in suspense,
to raise his mind to Him of whom they may possibly
be telling, to 'stand in awe and sin not,' and to ask
for light, yet to do no more; not boldly to put forward

what, if it be from God, yet has not been put forward
by Him. What He does in secret, we must think
over in secret; what He has openly showed in the
sight of the heathen, we must publish abroad, 'crying
aloud and sparing not.' An alleged miracle is not
untrue because it is unproved; nor is it excluded from
our faith because it is not admitted into our controversy.
Some are for our conviction, and these we are to
'confess with the mouth' as well as 'believe with the
heart'; others are for our comfort and encourage-
ment, and these we are to 'keep and ponder them
in our heart,' without urging them upon unwilling
ears." [1]

It seems to me that nothing could be more candid
or more reasonable than this statement—granting Dr.
Newman his general principle that all Scripture is
inspired as to matters of fact, so that Scripture narratives
of miracles stand on that ground, and on that ground
alone, on a different footing from all other such narratives. It is irrational in the highest degree for any
man who is absolutely convinced of the resurrection of
our Lord to ask for "legal" proofs of other miracles
of the same class, and manifesting the same character;
just as it would be irrational in the highest degree for
any man who knew a friend intimately to ask for legal
proofs that he was innocent of an alleged crime, before
believing him to be innocent of it. It may be perfectly
right in a Court of law to require legal proofs of guilt,
and when there are adequate legal proofs of guilt to
condemn the accused in the absence of any legal
disproof of their validity; but it is not right, it is pure

[1] *Two Essays on Scripture Miracles and on Ecclesiastical.*
Second edition, pp. 229, 230.

folly, for those who have far better evidence on the
subject within their reach than any Court of law can
have, to allow their judgment to be overruled by the
rules of a Court of law. The strict rules of legal evidence
are very valuable for those who have access to no better
evidence, but they rely, and rely rightly, on evidence
as much below the best to which the select few have
access, as it is above the best to which the world in
general has access. A man might just as well defer
to the rules of evidence accepted by a Court of law
in relation to a fact of which his own memory and conscience are (to him) the final and conclusive evidence,
as in relation to a fact of which his intimate knowledge
of a friend gave him far better assurance than any
evidence a Court of law could collect. It is simply a
truism to say that we should be highly unreasonable,
not specially reasonable, creatures, if we always demanded
legal proof before giving our hearty belief; and I think
that this applies even to specific miracles directly we
are satisfied of the existence of the class of events
called miracles, and of the moral and religious conditions under which the specific miracles are said to
have occurred. If I am convinced, as I heartily am,
of the resurrection of our Lord, to doubt that He stilled
the tempest, and raised the dead, when this is related
of Him by the same authorities and in the same spirit
in which His resurrection is recorded, seems to me not
a reasonable but a most unreasonable kind of doubt.
And yet this is the sort of doubt which Professor Huxley
expects us to foster in ourselves, only on the ground that
there would not be sufficient separate evidence of the
latter events if they stood quite apart, and in no organic
connection with the first. However, I am not arguing

the question, except so far as to show how candid and in every sense reasonable is Newman's mode of presenting it, and how utterly unjust it is to accuse him of laying down principles which place a great gulf between the ecclesiastical and the scientific mind. Professor Huxley's insinuation, that it is because miracles "may or have served a moral or religious end," that Newman encourages the belief in them is absolutely without a particle of foundation. It is not because they may serve, or have served, a moral or religious end that Newman regards them as more or less credible; but exclusively because they belong to a class of which the real existence has been proved by what he considers irrefragable evidence, that he demands a predisposition to accept them on sufficient external attestation, under any circumstances which bring them fairly within the conditions constituting that class. I suppose that if no one had ever heard of an active volcano, the accounts received of a great eruption such as took place a year or two ago in Java and Sumatra would be rightly received at first with extreme incredulity; and yet that, knowing what we do of those natural phenomena, there was no predisposition amongst scientific men to doubt the facts then narrated so long as there appeared to be clear individual testimony to those facts.

It is just the same with the Christian miracles. If the greatest of these rests on what Christians regard as overwhelming evidence, the lesser miracles are looked upon without any of that preliminary incredulity which we should rightly feel, if no event of the kind had ever been established to our satisfaction. All that Newman insists upon is, that "our feeling towards the ecclesiastical miracles turns much less on the evidence producible for

F

them, than on our view concerning their antecedent probability. If we think such interpositions of Providence likely, or not unlikely, there is quite enough evidence existing to convince us that they really do occur; if we think them as unlikely as they appear to Douglas, Middleton, and others, then even evidence as great as that which is producible for the miracles of Scripture would not be too much, nay, perhaps not enough, to conquer an inveterate, deep-rooted, and as it may be called, ethical incredulity." [1] And then he goes on to show, that those who believe that there is a special Divine presence in the Church, are predisposed to expect from that special Divine presence the same kind of effects as they had expected from the divinity of Christ, and had actually found in the records of His life. In fact, the whole "gulf" which exists, if any exists, between Dr. Newman and Professor Huxley, is described in the following sentence of the former : "The direct effect of evidence is to create a presumption, according to its strength, in favour of the fact attested; *it does not appear how it can create a presumption the other way.*" That is perfectly true, and is most pertinent where the defect of evidence is due, as in almost all historical cases, to the insufficient investigation which took place at the time, or to the loss of the records of that investigation, if there was investigation. But of course it does not apply to contemporary events where good evidence must usually have been producible, if it existed, and where it was challenged, but not produced. In that case the inadequacy of the evidence may amount to proof that good evidence does not exist at all, although if the

[1] *Two Essays on Scripture Miracles and on Ecclesiastical*, second edition, pp. 183-4.

alleged event had really happened, good evidence for it must have existed at the time. But Newman is confessedly arguing concerning the evidence of long past events, of which it would be impossible to assert that the slightness of the testimony actually adduced, furnished an indirect proof that there was no better evidence to give. It would be extremely difficult to imagine much slighter evidence than that which exists for the Trojan war as a real event; yet no one would say that, such as it is, it is of a kind to establish a presumption *unfavourable* to the reality of such a war. So far as it goes—and that is not far—it tends to create a presumption that there was such a war. And the same may be said for almost all the evidence, however slight and insufficient it may be, of which Newman is speaking. It is only when we know that adequate evidence must have existed, if the event happened at all, and that it was challenged and not forthcoming, that Newman's remark is untrue. It is not only true, but a truism in relation to events of which the records are more or less obliterated.

Where then is the trace of Newman's sceptical bias? It is impossible to furnish more abundant proof than his writings contain of his profound belief, first in the supernatural government of the world in general, next in the specially Divine revelation granted to the Jewish people, and lastly in the great fact of the incarnation, and of the foundation of a Church in which the same supernatural presence that was incarnate in Christ was immanent. He firmly believes that these antecedent convictions are essential for any due estimate of the miraculous element in the history of the Jewish and Christian Churches ; and though he

holds these convictions with all his heart, he still
appreciates with the soberest good sense the character
of the special evidence, or defect of evidence, for all the
alleged miracles which he examines. Would it have
furnished a better guarantee for Newman's Christian
faith if he had not sifted this special evidence with
the sobriety and discrimination which he has actually
displayed, for example, in reducing the alleged miracle
of "The Thundering Legion" to its true proportions?
On the contrary, it is precisely that sobriety and discrimination which wins a certain respect for his judgment when he expresses his belief as he does in relation to the well-attested failure of the Emperor Julian
to rebuild the Temple at Jerusalem, that there was
something in the story (as recounted by Julian's own
friend, and as a fragment of a letter from the hand of
the Emperor himself confirms it) of that fiery outbreak which prevented the rebuilding of the Temple,
beyond a mere strange coincidence; though of course
the concurrence of a great outburst of natural forces with
the expression of the Christian belief that the enterprise would fail, is regarded as a mere coincidence by all
sceptics.   There is nothing which so completely refutes
the theory of Newman's deep-rooted scepticism as the
clearness and candour with which he discusses and sums
up the evidence for and against mediæval miracles.

After all, the *gravamen* of the assertion, that Newman's nature is essentially sceptical, is to be found in
the heartiness and sincerity with which he accepted our
Lord's teaching, "Blessed are they who have not
seen, and yet have believed;" in other words, in his
belief that it is the predisposition to find what is Divine
in the world which enables us to discern it when it

comes within our range of experience. That is the true idealist philosophy, and not only the true idealist philosophy, but the true realist philosophy also. The mathematician finds in himself the principles which enable him to compute the courses of the planets, and the eclipses and occultations of the sun, moon, and stars; and if he had not had those principles within him, he would never have been able to declare what had taken place so many centuries before he was born, and what will take place for so many centuries after he is dead. The novelist and the dramatist finds in himself the key to the character of his fellow-men, and without that key would never be able to create for us so much which not only helps us to understand our fellow-men, but which positively adds to our knowledge of our own hearts. And so, too, the theologian would never find anything but an enigma in revelation, if he did not use the Divine anticipations which prompt him from within, to help him to unriddle the traces of Divine agency which he finds without. It is no more a disproof of miracles to say that as a rule they are only believed to happen by those who have a predisposition to believe, than it was a disproof of the existence of the American continent to say that it was only discovered by a navigator who was absolutely prepossessed with an almost unreasonably vehement conviction that it was there. And it seems to me that Newman could have given no more conclusive proof of the depth of his faith in the Christian revelation and the divinity of the ecclesiastical system, than the boldness with which he confronted the weak points in the evidence for the miracles, as well of Scripture as of ecclesiastical history, and demonstrated that his reason was as calm and

unbiased as his spirit was devout—nay, that in spite of
his disposition to expect Divine interpositions wherever
he recognized an undoubted indwelling of the Divine
presence, he was not disposed to ignore any distinct
evidence of exaggeration, confusion, and falsehood in
the records of these alleged interpositions.

CHAPTER VI.

BALANCING—DEFINING THE *VIA MEDIA*.

NEWMAN'S life at Oxford between 1833 and 1843 was no doubt in the main one of eager ecclesiastical propagandism, but after Hurrell Froude's death in 1836 it was certainly propagandism of a less confident kind. He was deeply convinced that the Anglican Church had a great work to do; that she had ignored her true work; that she had gone to sleep at her post; that she needed awakening to the duties she had neglected; and that if once she could be induced to claim her true position, not as an establishment, but as a Church, she might take a proud position in the Church of Christ. But in spite of the ardour, and sometimes, perhaps, the fierceness, as he called it, of his propagandism, especially while Hurrell Froude was still at his side, the irony with which he met his foes, the enthusiasm with which he supported his friends, there was probably not a month during the whole decade in which he was not more or less engaged in trying to define his position, to make out precisely what the theology of his Church really was, where he was standing, whose the authority was in the name of which he spoke. He was deeply convinced that, in regard to the worship of the Virgin

Mary, and the invocation of saints, Rome was in the
gravest error. He thought the Reformers in still graver
error in their view of the Sacraments. Yet he had
hard work to pilot himself and his party along that
"Via Media" which they wished to regard as the true
theology midway between Rome and Protestantism.
Almost all his books of the period remind me of the
soundings which are taken in the supposed neigh-
bourhood of land when a ship has run for several
days by the log alone, and has not been able to get the
altitude of the sun at noon. Then the lead is cast every
two or three minutes, while the cry of the number of
fathoms found is anxiously listened to by the ship's
crew and passengers.

I could not go carefully through the various publications of this period without prolonging this little book
to an unconscionable length. Some of them are too
technical to interest general readers, and very few of
them exhibit the rare literary power of Newman's later
works. But they all show the same conscientious and
almost morbid desire to clear up the theological position
of the party, though generally without any very satisfactory result. Newman intended, he says, to preach a
second and better Reformation, a return not to the sixteenth century, but to the seventeenth, to the theology
of Laud. "No time was to be lost, for the Whigs had
come to do their worst, and the rescue might come
too late. Bishoprics were already in course of sup-
pression; Church property was in course of confiscation;
sees would soon be receiving unsuitable occupants. We
knew enough to begin preaching upon, and there was
no one else to preach. I felt as on a vessel which
first gets under weigh, and then clears out the deck,

DEFINING THE *VIA MEDIA*.   73

and stores away luggage and live stock into the proper receptacles." [1]

At the same time, from the very first, amidst all the hurry to preach Church principles, there was at least an equal amount of self-questioning as to what precisely the new Church principles were to be. How were the Calvinistic elements in the Anglican Church to be dealt with, and minimized ? How were the authorities of the English Church to be persuaded that they ought to take a much higher stand than they had been accustomed to take, both against heresy and against the interference of the State ? How was the *Via Media* to be made so plain and impressive that the position of the renovated hier-archy should be clearly marked out, as against both Rome on the one side, and the representatives of the Reformers and the Erastians on the other ? In a word, though the movement went on merrily enough, Newman was constantly going through the process which the Germans call *Orientirung*—determining the true position of the new party, its precise latitude and longitude, so that it should be in no danger of being confounded with either Romanism or Protestantism.

One of the most remarkable, and certainly I think the most fascinating of all his efforts in this way, was the *Lectures on the Prophetical Office of the Church viewed relatively to Romanism and Popular Protestantism*, pub-lished in 1837, and since republished in the volumes entitled *The Via Media*.

It is an extremely characteristic as well as an ex-tremely subtle effort to discriminate the true view as to the use and abuse of private judgment, as to the

[1] *Apologia*, p. 113.

authority of the Church, and as to the authority of antiquity, and to discriminate these as well from the Roman Catholic view on the one side, as from the ordinary Protestant view on the other. He tells us quite frankly, that there are " conscientious and sensible men," who do not approve of the attempt he is making at all, on the ground that " though the views which may be put forward be in themselves innocent or true, yet under our circumstances they all lead to Rome, if only because the mind when once set in motion in any direction finds it difficult to stop ; and again, because the article of ' the Church ' has been accidentally the badge and index of that system." [1] As it turned out, these " conscientious and sensible men " showed themselves to be shrewd prophets. They knew how unlikely it was that such a Church as the Church of England, which was a political compromise between opposite tendencies from the day of its separation from Rome, could successfully assert for herself anything like a strong ecclesiastical independence, and what an advantage such a Church as the Church of Rome would have in competing with the Church of England for the guidance of minds which asked for a visible authority rather than for mere spiritual persuasiveness. Newman with his usual keenness saw the difficulties of his position better than he saw the way of surmounting them.

"Protestantism and Popery," he said in his Introductory Lecture, "are real religions; no one can doubt about them; they have furnished the mould in which nations have been cast; but the *Via Media*, viewed as an integral system, has never had existence except on

---

[1] *Via Media*, vol. i. p. 8.

paper; it is known not positively but negatively, in its differences from the rival creeds, not in its own properties; and can only be described as a third system, neither the one nor the other, but with something of each, cutting between them, and, as if with a critical fastidiousness, trifling with them both, and boasting to be nearer antiquity than either. What is this but to fancy a road over mountains and rivers which has never been cut? When we profess our *Via Media* as the very truth of the apostles, we seem to bystanders to be mere antiquarians or pedants, amusing ourselves with illusions or learned subtleties, and unable to grapple with things as they are." [1] Nevertheless, so profound was Newman's conviction that Romanism and popular Protestantism were both astray, that he was convinced that he should succeed in virtually making this "road over mountains and rivers," which hitherto had never been cut. It was a gallant enterprise, but one that, for all practical purposes, failed. The road was never made, though a track was marked out over the mountains, and fords were found across the rivers, practicable for a few adventurous men, and which are used by a certain number of stragglers even to the present day.

One of the best parts of the book was Newman's attack on that notion that it is a great privilege to judge for oneself on subjects on which one has no means of judging wisely for oneself—a privilege to which Englishmen assuredly cling tenaciously. He insists with great force, that to treat it as a mighty privilege that you should set out in life without any guidance is absurd in any field of thought and knowledge; but

---

[1] *Via Media*, vol. i. pp. 16, 17.

if absurd in every other field, it is most absurd of all
in the field of revelation, where it is so difficult to
apprehend clearly the true proportions of things, and
so easy to exaggerate one aspect of the Divine teaching
and to ignore or even suppress another. In maintaining his *Via Media* as to the function of private
judgment, and maintaining that it took an intermediate
course between trusting absolutely to the authority of
a Church which settles everything by its *fiat,* and the
ultra-Protestant principle which pretends that every
Christian should be able to make out from his Bible
alone what has been revealed, Newman asserts that to use
private judgment properly you must *begin* with the habit
of obedience to those who have " natural authority " over
you, no matter who they are ; and must cultivate a teach-
able temper before you dare to cavil and scrutinize.
The very best sort of investigation, he maintains, is
conducted half unconsciously, without any pride in it,
and without any fuss about it. People who boast of
their exercise of the right of private judgment seldom
exercise it in the right spirit, which cannot be one of
ostentatious satisfaction at the use of such a liberty,
since it should be one of eagerness to get at the truth,
while eagerness to get at the truth implies eagerness
to avail yourself of any help that will really serve your
purpose—in other words, implies eagerness to give up
your liberty to an experienced and honest guide. Those
who say to themselves, " I am examining, I am scru-
tinizing, I am judging, I am free to choose or reject, I
am exercising the right of Private Judgment," are
indulging in a very strange kind of satisfaction, like the
satisfaction of a person who exults in his grief for a
friend, and says, " I am weeping ; I am overcome and

agonized for the second or third time ; I am resolved
to weep." [1] A person who said that would not be
credited with feeling very deeply ; and it is an equally
strange infatuation, in Newman's mind, to boast of
being without an opinion, and of being determined to
find the truth without aid. " Who would boast," he
asks, " that he was without worldly means, and had
to get them as he could ? Is heavenly treasure less
precious than earthly ? Is it anything inspiring or
consolatory to consider, as such persons do, that
Almighty God has left them entirely to their own
efforts, has failed to interpret their wants, has let them
lose in ignorance at least a considerable part of their
short life, and their tenderest and most malleable years ?
Is it a hardship or a yoke, on the contrary, to be told
that what, in the order of Providence, is put before them
to believe, whether absolutely true or not, is in such
sense from Him, that it will inspire their hearts to obey
it, and will convey to them many truths which they
otherwise could not know, and prepare them perhaps
for the comunication of higher and clearer views ? " [2] In
short, private judgment, according to Newman, is at its
best when it is working half unconsciously to realize
the full meaning of what has been impressed upon it, and
is not so much the attitude of a mind sitting in judgment,
as of a mind striving earnestly to apprehend and piece
together the lessons it has learned from many different
quarters, without asserting any arbitrary liberty or
falling into any defiant attitude. Reverence and
humility are, in Newman's view, the just conditions of
the right exercise of private judgment, and you cannot

---

[1] *Via Media*, vol. i. p. 137.   [2] *Ibid*. vol. i. p. 137.

have these conditions for forming your judgment under
the most favourable form without a Church that has
authority, but does not overstrain that authority. " If
Scripture-reading," he says, " has in England been the
cause of schism, it is because we are deprived of the
power of excommunicating, which in the revealed
scheme is the formal antagonist and curb of Private
Judgment." [1] Rome, on the other hand, does not sufficiently train the members of her communion to compare the Scriptures with her teaching, but imposes her
teaching on them too absolutely as that of an infallible
Church, which may dictate without any attempt to
elicit and secure her children's individual apprehension
and assent. Newman charges Rome with being too
intellectual, too systematic in the theology she imposes.
Rome professes to take a complete survey and make a
complete map of the region of Divine mysteries, and so
falls into the same error as the Scotch Presbyterianism,
for instance, which, from a very different point of view,
commits the same fault.

" When religion is reduced in all its parts to a system,
there is hazard of something earthly being made the
chief object of our contemplation instead of our Maker.
Now Rome classifies our duties and their reward, the
things to believe, the things to do, the modes of pleasing
God, the penalties and the remedies of sin, with such
exactness that an individual knows (so to speak) just
where he is upon his journey heavenward, how far he has
got, how much he has to pass; and his duties become a
matter of calculation." [2] Now the *Via Media* between
the absoluteness of the Roman Church and the self-

---

[1] *Via Media*, vol. i. p. 140.
[2] *Ibid.* p. 102.

will of many of the Protestant sects, which sometimes
results in a system as definite and sharply defined, is
the comparatively gentle authority of a Church which
elicits and even cultivates the spirit of freedom in
its children, but curbs it and will not allow it to go
beyond a certain point in asserting either freedom of
opinion or freedom of practice. Newman held that
the infallibility which Rome claims not only makes her
arrogant towards the private judgment of her children,
but also encourages an arrogance in her dealings with
" the deposit of truth" committed to her, and with the
earliest traditions of the Church, that leads to virtual
indifference to the authority of antiquity, and in fact
to a breach with its traditions. And this he held that
Rome had done in relation to the doctrine both of Purgatory and Indulgences, as well as in relation to the
doctrine of Infallibility itself. He accused the Church
of Rome of hardly even affecting to produce a formal
proof of her infallibility, the dogma being " serviceable
in practice though extravagant in theory." He thought
the Roman claim of infallibility to be rather like the
political maxim that " the king can do no wrong,"
" which vividly expresses some great and necessary
principle," [1] though not of course attempting any argu-
mentative proof. " A teacher who claims infallibility is
readily believed on his simple word." The Roman
Church, he thought, rids herself of competition by fore-
stalling it. " And probably in the eyes of her children
this is not the least persuasive argument for her infallibility, that she alone of all Churches dares claim
it, as if a secret instinct and involuntary misgivings

[1] *Via Media*, vol. i. p. 117.

restrained those rival communions which go so far towards affecting it." [1]

In the preface to the third edition of this book, published after Newman became a Roman Catholic, and in the notes appended to the Anti-Romanist portion of this volume, Newman of course retracts what he had said of the arrogance and presumption of the Roman Church, and intimates that he had spoken rather because he had confidence in the Anglican divines of the seventeenth century, whom he followed in making these statements, than because he had verified for himself all their charges against Rome. These charges were necessary, he says, to the position of the Anglican Church; and though he believed them to be true, he believed them rather on tradition than on his own knowledge. He had but partially examined the controversy, but he accepted, as he was bound to do, the authority of the divines of his own Church on its merits. In fact, he had acted on his own principle in relation to private judgment, he had accepted the bias of those whom he regarded as his proper teachers, and had only partially verified their statements for himself.

It is sometimes intimated that this assumption of the truth of charges which Newman had not fully examined savoured of that tone of mind which implies not so much a profound conviction that a creed is true, as a willing *assent* to its truth, of which the Roman Catholics are specially accused. And if it be a fitting subject for accusation, I think it is a just accusation; but I doubt whether it is a fitting subject for it at all.

[1] *Via Media*, p. 117.

If any man examines his real creed on any subject whatever, religious, moral, political, or psychological, he will
find that there are in it a few articles of deep personal
conviction, on which he may be truly said to be one of
those adherents who help to diffuse them, but a great
many articles which he accepts only because they have
usually been held in connection with those on which his
own conviction is earnest, and are held by those for whose
general tone of mind he feels a deep respect, and from
intercourse with whom he has learned the greater part
of his own religious or moral or political or psychological creed.

For instance, Newman believed with all his heart, as
an article of deep personal conviction, that an organized
Church was necessary both to interpret Scripture
and to administer the Sacraments ordained by our
Lord, but he accepted almost passively as a part of
the creed of those Anglican divines who had inspired
him with this conviction, the opinion that Purgatory
and the Invocation of Saints are not only non-scriptural
but non-primitive, and cannot be identified as beliefs
of the early Church at all; and again, that Rome, relying
on her own assumed infallibility, had early become
quite careless as to the origin of her traditions, and
had allowed herself to sanction beliefs which she could
not trace back to the times of the Apostles, or even
of the apostolic fathers. He knew enough to know
that nothing could be more plausible than such a
position. He did not know enough to be sure that he
should always hold it on the strength of the historical
evidence alone; but if he is to be very seriously blamed
for advancing it, as all his Anglican predecessors had
advanced it, I think there is hardly a controversialist

G

in the world who will not be liable to blame of the same kind. I suppose the truth to be, that there is no Scriptural evidence worthy of the name, and but little evidence in the records of the primitive Church, for the doctrines and practices which Newman and the great Anglican divines of the seventeenth century condemned as Romanizing innovations on the doctrines and practices of the Apostolic Church, but that there is enough trace of them in comparatively early writings to convince those who are otherwise assured of the need of a single authority to determine controversy, that the Romanists have a fair case for asserting that these traditions have a root in the early past.

These are points on which it is quite easy for those who cannot believe in an infallible Church to feel assured that the *soi-disant* infallible Church has used her assumed infallibility to add to the faith of the Apostles ; while it is equally easy for those who cannot believe that any Church whose authority on any matter of creed is less than absolute, is a Church worthy of the name, to accept as sufficient evidence of an undeveloped germ of doctrine or usage what those whose attitude of mind was different would regard as evidence utterly unworthy of serious notice. Newman's craving for a final human authority on matters of dogma made rapid strides between 1837, when these lectures on the Roman and Protestant controversy were written, and 1845, when he joined the Church of Rome. It is very natural, and not, I think, a matter for censure, that his estimate of the evidence for the primitiveness of the Roman Catholic creed changed to some extent as his sense of the necessity for some final tribunal in these matters steadily grew.

. A very much less interesting book than *The Prophetical Office of the Church* was the *Lectures on
Justification by Faith,* published in 1838, which I confess I have found somewhat straw-chopping and dry.
It is an attempt to show that, while the Roman theology
is right in making sanctification the substance of
justification, the Lutheran and Anglican theology is
yet right in making justification (by which Newman
means not *making* man just, but *accounting* him just)
the initial stage, and sanctification only the necessary
consequence of justification. It is, I think, very
difficult for a layman of this generation to enter into
the interest of this controversy at all. Even laymen
can fully understand the magic of faith, how new and
how potent a motive is furnished to man's life the
moment they can discern a really Divine nature in
which they may implicitly trust for the guidance of
their hearts and wills. But none the less they often
find it both difficult and unprofitable to enter into
the finer distinctions which St. Paul has been supposed
to draw between the various stages of the Divine
change, and especially the "imputation" of righteousness, or "accounting righteous," which, according to
Lutheran divines, precedes the *making* righteous. All
they know is that faith is a renovating principle in the
highest sense; but it does not seem to them of the
highest moment to discern whether, between the gift
of faith and the resulting spiritual renovation, there is
or is not wedged in this somewhat unreal and, as it
seems, at first sight at all events, fictitious declaration,
that they are already *accounted* in the sight of God
what they only hope to become. Newman says, with
what seems unanswerable force, in these lectures,

" Strange it is, but such is the opinion of one of the two schools of divinity which have all along been mentioned, that God's calling us righteous implies not only that we have not been, but that we never shall be righteous. Surely it is a strange paradox to say that a thing is not, because He says it is; that the solemn averment of the living and true God is inconsistent with the fact averred ; that His accepting our obedience is a bar to His making it acceptable ; and that the glory of His pronouncing us righteous lies in His leaving us unrighteous." [1] Strange indeed, and more than incredible, intolerable to piety. But even Newman's own statement of the case, though not open to the charge of being so intolerably paradoxical as this horrible doctrine, is to my mind full of difficulty. "Justification," he says, "is 'the glorious voice of the Lord' declaring us to be righteous. That it is a declaration, not a making, is sufficiently clear from this one argument, that it is the justification of a *sinner*, of one who *has been* a sinner; and the past cannot be reversed except by *accounting* it reversed. Nothing can bring back time bygone; nothing can undo what is done. God treats us *as if* that had not been which has been; that is, by a merciful economy or representation, He says of us as to the past, what in fact is otherwise than what He says it is. It is true that justification extends to the present as well as to the past; yet if so, still in spite of this it must mean an imputation or declaration, or it would cease to have respect to the past. And if it once be granted to mean an imputation, it cannot mean anything else, for it

---

[1] *Lectures on the Doctrine of Justification,* 3rd edition, p. 78.

cannot have two meanings at once. To account and to make are perfectly distinct ideas. The subject-matter may be double, but the act of justification is one; what it is as to the past, such must it be as to the present; it is a declaration about the past, it is a declaration about the present."[1] And then he goes on to illustrate his meaning thus : " In the fourth chapter of his Epistle to the Romans St. Paul makes justification synonymous with '*imputing* righteousness,' and quotes David's words concerning the blessedness of those 'whose iniquities are forgiven, and whose sins are covered,' and ' to whom the Lord will not impute sin.' Righteousness then is the name, character, or estimation of righteousness vouchsafed to the past, and extending from the past to the present, as far as the present is affected by the past. It is the accounting a person not to have that present guilt, peril, odiousness, ill-repute with which the past actually burdens him. If a wrong has been done you, and you forgive the offender, you count it as though it had not been, you pass it over. You view him as before he did it, and treat him as on his original footing. You consider him to have been what he has not been, fair and friendly towards you ; that is, you impute righteousness to him or justify him. When a parent forgives a child, it is on the same principle. He says, ' I will think no more of it this time ; I will forget what has happened ; I will give you one more trial.' In this sense it is all one to say that he forgives the child, or that he counts him to have been and to be a good child, and treats him as if he had not been disobedient. He declares him dutiful, and thereby

[1] *Lectures on Justification*, p. 67.

indirectly forgives that past self which lives in his
present self and makes him a debtor." But the
illustration seems to me to tell entirely against the
doctrine that imputation is a sort of legal fiction. The
father forgives the child in the confidence that by
relying on the child's better self, and showing him that
he trusts that better self, he will fortify and strengthen
the better self against the worse. Neither the child
nor the father supposes for a moment that the recol-
lection of the act of disobedience is really blotted out,
or that there is any fictitious hypothesis in the case.
The child knows that the first disobedience is not to
be brought up against him so long as he acts on
the higher spirit which has regained the victory, and
that simply for the reason that the father's renewed
trust is itself a renovating power, and far more potent
than the principle of fear. And that is, I suppose,
what is meant in the 32nd Psalm by the Lord's not
imputing iniquity, for the passage runs : "Blessed is
he whose transgression is forgiven, whose sin is covered.
Blessed is the man unto whom the Lord imputeth not
iniquity, and *in whose spirit there is no guile ;*" in other
words, who is really purified from evil by the trust
which God places in him. It does not seem to me
that there is any trace here of a legal fiction at all.
The reason God does not impute iniquity is because
He sees the change of heart which grace and faith
have made, because He sees that at last " in his spirit
there is no guile." There is no taking for granted that
the man to whom the Lord will not impute iniquity
has been sinless, there is only a declaration of the
intention to trust the renovated spirit in him as the
best and highest means of strengthening that spirit.

The former struggle is recognized; the defeat is recognized; the renewal of the struggle and the victory are recognized; and the Divine trust is promised by way of securing that victory. Newman believes, of course, that the "accounting just" is followed by the being just. I should have thought that God would not, and could not, declare any man just till he was just, and that the being just must precede the Divine declaration that he is just. Nor, so far as I can see, does Newman make the matter any clearer by the following explanation of it. "God's word," he says, "effects what it announces. This is its characteristic all through Scripture. He 'calleth those things which be not as though they are,' and they are forthwith. Thus in the beginning He *said*, 'Let there be light, and there was light.' Word and deed went together in creation; and so again 'in the regeneration,' '*The Lord gave the word, great was the company of the preachers.*' So again in His miracles, He *called* Lazarus from the grave, and the dead arose; He *said* 'Be thou cleansed,' and the leprosy departed; He *rebuked* the winds and the waves, and they were still; He *commanded* the evil spirits, and they fled away; He said to St. Peter, St. Andrew, St. John, St. James, and St. Matthew, 'Follow Me,' and they arose, 'for His word was with power.' And so again in the sacraments, His word is the consecrating principle. As He blessed the loaves and fishes, and they multiplied, so He 'blessed and brake,' and the bread became His Body."[1] And that would all be applicable if what was asserted by these theologians were, that at God's word "Let the soul be just," it became just. But what they

----

[1] *Lectures on Justification*, 3rd edition, p. 81.

say is, that He *declares* it to be just while it is still unjust, and by "accounting" it what it is not, by imputing to it qualities which it has not, He makes it what He had assumed it to be. This seems to me a wholly artificial sort of language, and one which tends towards the depreciation of inspired teaching, not towards its exaltation. The drift of the lectures on justification is to show that justification must issue in sanctification; but the Catholic doctrine that what justifies is either grace or charity, and that these are different names for the same reality,—grace being the word which tells us whence the gift comes, and charity the word which tells us what manner of life it causes,— seems to me much nearer the truth than any form of the Lutheran doctrine. The lectures were indeed an elaborate effort to reconcile the Lutheran view of this subject with the Catholic view, and constituted the application of the conception of the *Via Media* to the special subject of faith and its regenerating effects on the soul.

A much more interesting effort of Newman's to reconcile his position with Anglican doctrine was his attempt to show, in the lectures on *Holy Scripture in Relation to the Catholic Creed*, that there is no more difficulty in proving from Scripture the Church doctrines he was preaching than there was in proving from Scripture the doctrine of the Trinity, and much less than in proving the authenticity of the canon. These lectures were published in 1838 as Tract 85 of the famous *Tracts for the Times*, and are even more charac- teristic of Newman's mind and method at that time than the much more famous Tract 90. He begins by putting very strongly the difficulty in which those persons are placed who desire to believe in the authority of the

Anglican Church, and who have yet been taught by her that all her doctrines may be proved from Scripture. " They find that the proof is *rested* by us on Scripture, and therefore they require more explicit *Scripture proof*. They say, ' All this that you say about the Church is very specious and very attractive ; but where is it to be found in the inspired volume ? ' And that it is *not* found there (that is, I mean, not found as fully as it might be), seems to them proved at once by the simple fact that all persons (I may say all, for the exceptions are very few)—all those who try to form their creed by Scripture only—fall away from the Church and her doctrines, and join one or other sect and party, as if showing, that whatever is or is not scriptural, at least the Church, by consent of all men, is not so." [1] Newman admits that he had felt this difficulty very keenly himself, and says he regards it as " one of the main difficulties, and (as I think) one of the intended difficulties, which God's providence puts at this day in the path of those who seek Him, for purposes known or unknown, ascertainable or not." [2] But great as the difficulty is, he states his conviction that, as he has otherwise most abundant proof of " the Divine origin of the Church system of doctrine," as of apostolical succession and the sacramental system which depends upon it, he ought not to be in any way dismayed because the evidence, though given also in Scripture, " might be given more explicitly and fully, and (if I may so say) more consistently."

This introduction to the lectures seems to me a virtual admission that without the evidence of ecclesiastical history and tradition *outside* Scripture, Newman

---

[1] *Tract* 85, p. 2. [2] *Ibid.* p. 2.

could never have found *in* Scripture adequate proof
of the Church system. He did find it there when
the history of the primitive Church had drawn his
attention to the manner in which that Church understood and acted upon Scripture, but without the
aid of that practical commentary, he clearly admits,
I think, that Scripture would not have furnished him
with adequate proof of the Church system. In dealing
with the difficulty, he begins by owning that the
general drift of his argument is of a kind to make him
somewhat anxious as to its effect. Its tendency is to
show that those who give up Church principles because
they are not explicitly taught in Scripture, ought to
give up other principles too which have always been
held to be of the very essence of revelation; and he
admits his reluctance to push any argument which may
have the effect *not* of making those who do not now
hold Church principles accept them, but of making
them give up Christian doctrines which they had hitherto confidently held. "When I show a man that he is
inconsistent," he says, "I make him decide whether of
the two he loves better—the portion of truth or the
portion of error which he already holds. If he loves
the truth better, he will abandon the error; if the
error, he will abandon the truth. And this is a fearful
and anxious trial to put him under, and one cannot but
feel loth to have recourse to it. One feels that perhaps
it may be better to keep silence, and to allow him, in
shallowness and presumption, to assail one's own position
with impunity, than to retort, however justly, his weapons
on himself; better for oneself to seem a bigot, than to
make him a scoffer."[1]   But, serious as he feels this

[1] *Tract* 85, pp. 3, 4.

difficulty to be, he holds that on the whole it avails only "for the cautious use, not for the abandonment, of the argument in question. For it is our plain duty to push and defend the truth in a straightforward way. Those who are to stumble must stumble rather than the heirs of grace should not hear." Therefore, though he admits frankly that when his argument *has* effect, it may have either a bad effect or a good, he has so much more confidence in the good effect it will have on men who love the truth, than in the bad effect it may have on men who love their own opinion, that he thinks it his duty to push home the argument that Scripture, if it does not explicitly establish Church doctrines, does not explicitly establish even the universally received Christian doctrines, in order that he may induce those who are disposed to Church principles to accept them frankly on implicit rather than on explicit Scripture testimony. And then Newman explains candidly what he finds to be the only Scripture testimony to two leading Church doctrines.

While Baptism and its spiritual benefits are often mentioned in the Epistles, "its peculiarity as the one plenary remission of sin" "is not insisted on with such frequency and earnestness as might be expected,—chiefly in one or two passages of our Epistles, and these obscurely (in Heb. vi. and x.). Again, the doctrine of Absolution is made to rest on but one or two texts (in Matt. xvi. and John xx.), with little or no practical exemplification of it in the Epistles, where it was to be expected. 'Why,' it may be asked, 'are not the Apostles continually urging their converts to rid themselves of sin after Baptism as best they can, by penance, confession, absolution, satisfaction? Again, why are Christ's

ministers nowhere called priests, or at most in one or
two obscure passages (as in Rom. xv.) ? ' " [1]

And after a number of similar questions, comes
Newman's mode of meeting the difficulty, which is
to show that if we are to accept only what is plainly
and consistently enforced in Scripture, we should
have to sacrifice not only what are called Church
doctrines, but external worship altogether, to accept
Christ's saying, that the hour cometh when neither
in Samaria nor at Jerusalem the Father shall be
worshipped, as prohibiting all external rites, and
forbidding them in principle; as denying all benefit
from the Eucharist, or from Baptism, or from public
worship itself. On "*how many* special or palmary texts
do any of the doctrines or rites we hold depend ? What
doctrines or rites would be left to us if we demanded
the clearest and fullest evidence before we believed
anything ? " [2] Newman's drift is, that if that sort of
Scripture evidence were required for every doctrine and
rite, nothing of Christianity would be left beyond at
most what the Latitudinarians are willing to concede.
By Latitudinarianism Newman means the view that it
is not at all important what doctrine a man holds, so
long as he acts up conscientiously to whatever doctrine
he does honestly hold. That is a view which Newman
thinks simply absurd as a view of *Revelation*. It might
be an adequate view of natural religion, but when God
reveals Himself, it is obvious that He does attach great
importance to the substance of the revelation given,
and that He cannot possibly be indifferent *what* a man
believes concerning Him, since He has provided so

[1] *Tract* 85, pp. 5, 6.   [2] *Ibid.* p. 12.

elaborate an agency for giving him a true belief, or at
least a much truer belief than he had before, or than,
by the mere light of nature, he could have obtained.
" There is an overpowering improbability," he says,
" in Almighty God's announcing that He has revealed
something, and revealing nothing; there is no antecedent
improbability in His revealing it elsewhere than in an
inspired volume." [1]   Hence, if Newman had to choose
between Latitudinarianism and Roman Catholicism, he
would have chosen the latter as far the more rational
of the two views of revelation to any one who was
convinced that a revelation had been made.   Still he
thought that the doctrine of the *Via Media*, that Scripture does reveal with sufficient clearness the whole
Church system, if you will consent to look at what it
implies, as well as at what it explicitly states, was quite
tenable; but that Latitudinarianism, or indifference to
doctrine so long as a man acted honestly on his own
view, was utterly untenable.

Newman never seemed to think that the unveiling
of God's own *character* was, after all, the main purpose
of revelation, and that that might possibly be adequately accomplished without the aid of any elaborate
Church system, or any great network of doctrine over
and above the evidence of what God had actually
done in order to embody that character in a human
life and personality.   To Newman's mind, the "dogmatic system" on which he insists, always seems to
me to overshadow somewhat the central truth of revelation—the truth as to the character of God, and the
significance of that truth as displayed in what He

[1] *Tract* 85, p. 19.

had done for men. It is surely not nearly so certain
that any elaborately ramified "system" has been
revealed to us, as it is that God's character has been
emphatically revealed in what the Son of God was and
did for mankind.

Nothing can be more remarkable than the way in
which Newman illustrates the principle that if you
look only to the surface of Scripture, you find not only
no adequate evidence for many of the greater Christian
doctrines, but no adequate evidence for the inspiration
of Scripture itself, and still more, no adequate evidence
for the exact contents of revelation, for what Scripture
consists of, for what is properly included in the canon.
He described in a most graphic passage the apparently
accidental character of the contents of Scripture. "It is
as if you were to seize the papers or correspondence of
leading men in any school of philosophy or science which
were never designed for publication, and bring them out
in one volume. You would find probably in the collection
so resulting many papers begun and not finished; some
parts systematic and didactic, but the greater part
made up of hints or of notices which assume first principles instead of asserting them, or of discussions upon
particular points which happened to require their
attention. I say the doctrines, the first principles, the
rules, the objects of the school would be taken for
granted, alluded to, implied, not stated. You would
have some trouble to get at them; you would have
many repetitions, many hiatuses, many things which
looked like contradictions; you would have to work
your way through heterogeneous materials, and after
your best efforts there would be much hopelessly
obscure; and on the other hand, you might look in

vain in such a casual collection for some particular
opinions which the critics are known, nevertheless, to
have held, nay, to have insisted on." [1]

Such is, he says, with some limitations, the character
of Scripture, which is not only an apparently miscellaneous collection of writings, but one of which we
only know that the primitive Church had sifted it
out, and believed this to be the authentic collection,
though why these books were accepted and others
rejected we do not know. But what Newman infers
from this is not that this account of the Bible is the
true account, but that there is obviously a great deal
beneath the letter of the Bible which we can only get
at by trusting the authority of the Church, the same
authority by which alone confessedly the canon of Scripture was determined. He regards all these criticisms on
Scripture as proving not that it is what it seems to be
at first sight, but that it is much deeper than what
it seems to be at first sight, and what only the Church
has adequately disclosed to us. His general inference
from his examination is, that "whether this or that
doctrine, this or that book of Scripture, is fully provable
or not, that line of objection to them cannot be right
which when pursued destroys Church, Creed, Bible
altogether—which obliterates the very Name of Christ
from the world." [2] His view evidently was, that there
is something analogous in the apparently accidental and
miscellaneous character of Scripture to the apparently
accidental and miscellaneous character of human life,
which, though it is governed in every detail by Providence, and meant for the discipline and probation of

---

[1] *Tract* 85, pp. 30—31.   [2] *Ibid.* pp. 100.

man, seems to be so full of what is unintentional, and what does not bear upon the discipline and probation of man. The Church reveals a hidden unity and purpose within Scripture, just as Scripture reveals a hidden unity and purpose in human life, and the true Christian has to choose between accepting this hidden unity and purpose in deference to the teaching of the Church, and entering on a course of destructive criticism which must end in breaking down the belief in revelation itself, and leaving nothing of the least value for our faith to apprehend. His whole drift was, that the Church can verify its credentials out of Scripture if men will follow her guidance in first accepting as Scripture what she has given them, and then looking devoutly for the true meaning of Scripture where she tells them to look for it; but that without this humility and trust in the Church, Scripture alone will fail us, and yield up incoherent or capricious meanings, varying with the minds of those who take upon themselves the task of interpreting it.

CHAPTER VII.

NEWMAN AT ST. MARY'S.

FROM 1828 to 1843 Newman was vicar of St. Mary's, as well as chaplain of Littlemore, and preached in the pulpit of St. Mary's those *Parochial and Plain Sermons* by which perhaps he has influenced the world more deeply, though not perhaps more widely, than it has ever fallen to any Englishman of our time to influence it through the instrumentality of the pulpit. Mr. Gladstone has described Newman's manner in the pulpit in a speech on preaching, which he delivered at the City Temple in 1887. "When I was an under-graduate of Oxford," he said, "Dr. Newman was looked upon rather with prejudice as what is termed a Low Churchman, but was very much respected for his character and his known ability. Without ostentation or effort, but by simple excellence, he was constantly drawing undergraduates more and more around him. Now Dr. Newman's manner in the pulpit was one about which, if you considered it in its separate parts, you would arrive at very unsatisfactory conclusions. There was not very much change in the inflexion of the voice; action there was none. His sermons were read, and his eyes were always bent on his book; and all that,

H

you will say, is against efficiency in preaching. Yes, but you must take the man as a whole, and there was a stamp and a seal upon him; there was a solemn sweetness and music in the tone; there was a complete-ness in the figure, taken together with the tone and with the manner, which made even his delivery, such as I have described it, and though exclusively from written sermons, singularly attractive."

I should very much doubt if Newman could ever have been properly described as a Low Churchman after he became the vicar of St. Mary's in 1828. He himself tells us in his *Apologia*, that between 1822 and 1825 he was fully under the influence of Dr. Hawkins, afterwards the Provost of Oriel, from whom he learned the doctrines of Baptismal Regeneration, and the relation between Scripture and tradition, as moderate High Churchmen understood that relation. Indeed, the first of the two sermons belonging to the year 1828 is a sermon on Baptismal Regeneration, and I do not think it possible that any one who held the views therein set down could properly be described as a Low Churchman. Moreover, on the appearance of *The Christian Year* in 1827, Newman adopted at once and enthusiastically the sacramental system as it was set forth in *The Christian Year*, and from 1828, when he was first made vicar of St. Mary's, he became one of Keble's intimate friends and, as one may say, disciples. Hence it is clear, I think, that Newman's reputed Low Churchmanship must have been in 1828 the mere vestige of the character by which he was at first known at Oxford, and not in any respects a true reflection of the teaching to which he gave utterance in the pulpit of his own church. Newman when vicar of St. Mary's must be

regarded, I think, as a representative of high ecclesiastical views from the very first. But I need not say
that it was not this characteristic of his which gained
him the eager attention of the Oxford undergraduates.
The very first characteristic about the parochial sermons
of this vicar of St. Mary's is, that they are so clear
and so emphatic in their recognition of the actual
facts of life.

Take as an illustration what may well have been one
of the very first sermons preached by him as vicar of
St. Mary's on "Religion a weariness to the natural
man" (July 27th, 1828, sermon 2 of vol. vii.). Consider
the calmness with which he sets the facts of the case
before his hearers. "Putting aside for an instant the
thought of the ingratitude and the sin which indifference to Christianity implies, let us, as far as we dare,
view it merely as a matter of fact, after the manner of
the text, and form a judgment on the probable consequences of it; let us take the state of the case as it is
proved, and survey it dispassionately, as even an un-
believer might survey it, without at the moment considering whether it is sinful or not; as a misfortune,
if we will, or a strange accident, or a necessary condition
of our nature—one of the phenomena, as it may be
called, of the present world." That is just the way to
take the ears of young men, to tell them that you want
to put edification for a moment aside, and to face the
facts of the world as they are, without moralizing or
preaching. Then how vividly he describes the feelings
of the young about religion. "The very terms 'religion,'
'devotion,' 'piety,' 'conscientiousness,' 'mortification,'
and the like you find to be inexpressibly dull and
cheerless; you cannot find fault with them, indeed you

would if you could; and whenever the words are explained in particulars and realized, then you do find
occasion for exception and objection. But though you
cannot deny the claims of religion used as a vague and
general term, yet how irksome, cold, uninteresting, un-
inviting does it at best appear to you! how severe its
voice! how forbidding its aspect! With what animation,
on the contrary, do you enter into the mere pursuits
of time and the world! What bright anticipations of
joy and happiness flit before your eyes! How you are
struck and dazzled at the view of the prizes of this life,
as they are called! How you admire the elegancies
of art, the brilliance of wealth, or the force of intellect!
According to your opportunities, you mix in the world,
you meet and converse with persons of various conditions and pursuits, and are engaged in the number-
less occurrences of daily life. You are full of news;
you know what this or that person is doing, and what
has befallen him; what has not happened, which was
near happening, what may happen. You are full of
ideas and feelings upon all that goes on around you.
But from some cause or other religion has no part, no
sensible influence, in your judgment of men and things.
It is out of your way. Perhaps you have your pleasure
parties; you readily take your share in them time after
time; you pass continuous hours in society where you
know that it is quite impossible even to mention the
name of religion. Your heart is in scenes and places
where conversation on serious subjects is strictly forbidden by the rules of the world's propriety." [1]

Nothing could be more characteristic of Newman's

---

[1] *Parochial and Plain Sermons,* vol. vii. A new edition, pp.
17, 18. Rivingtons, 1868.

preaching than the passage in which he reminds his
hearers how greatly they enjoy the little thrill of
excitement which accompanies news-telling, nay, not
merely news-telling, but telling what, under certain
conditions which were "very near happening," but did
not happen, the news *might* have been though it was
not; and in what strange contrast this thrill of pleasure-
able interest in imparting to others the tidings of what
might have been as much as a ripple in the stream of
time (though in fact it was not even a ripple), stands
to the dismay and weariness with which the mere
mention of eternal interests is regarded. That profound
reality of mind was one of the most important of the
characteristics which made Newman's preaching so
potent an influence at Oxford.

Again, nothing is more striking—it is indeed another
aspect of this same reality of mind—than Newman's
constant anxiety not to exaggerate at all in his delinea-
tions of human weakness and frivolousness. In the
sermon on the duty of self-denial, preached in the Lent
of 1830, he describes the preoccupations of ordinary
society in a light not very different from that of the
sermon I have just quoted; but observe how anxious
he is not in the least to exceed the truth. "You may
go into mixed society; you will hear men conversing
on their friend's prospects, openings in trade, or realized
wealth, on his advantageous situation, the pleasant con-
nections he has formed, the land he has purchased, the
house he has built; then they amuse themselves with
conjecturing what this or that man's property may be,
where he lost, where he gained, his shrewdness or his
rashness, or his good fortune in this or that speculation.
Observe, I do not say that such conversation is wrong;

I do not say that we must always have on our lips the
very thoughts which are deepest in our hearts, or that
it is safe to judge of individuals by such speeches; but
when this sort of conversation is the customary standard
conversation of the world, and when a line of conduct
answering to it is the prevalent conduct of the world
(and this is the case), is it not a grave question for each
of us, as living in the world, to ask himself what abiding
notion we have of the necessity of self-denial, and how
far we are clear of the danger of resembling that evil
generation which ' ate and drank, which married wives,
and were given in marriage, which bought and sold,
planted and builded, till it rained fire and brimstone
from heaven and destroyed them all." ' [1] In the studious
guardedness of this criticism of the world's ways lies
more than half the impressiveness and power of this
sermon.

It is impossible to speak of the extraordinary reality
of Newman's sermons at St. Mary's without referring
especially to the wonderful sermon preached on the
2nd June, 1839, on "Unreal Words." To more than
one living man that sermon has, I believe, been one of
the greater influences governing the conduct of their life
—I mean, of course, their interior life as well as their
external conduct. The teaching that under the Christian
Revelation we are "no longer in the region of shadows,"
that as the true light shines we are bound to avail
ourselves of it and make all our professions and words
real, and yet that nothing is so rare as reality and
singleness of mind, and that we ought to test our own
sincerity as Christ so often tested the sincerity of those

---

[1] *Parochial and Plain Sermons*, vol. vii. p. 88.

who made great professions to Him, is enforced with a
freshness and dramatic insight that makes the sermon
unforgettable. The whole effect of it is to make its
readers feel how easy it is to be unconsciously insincere.
Newman does not want "to hinder us from obeying,"
but "to sober us in professing." "To make professions,"
he says, "is to play with edged tools, unless we attend
to what we are saying. Words have a meaning, whether
we mean that meaning or not; and they are imputed
to us in their real meaning when our not meaning it is
our own fault."[1]

This is the sense in which Newman understands
our Lord's saying, "By thy words thou shalt be
justified, and by thy words thou shalt be condemned." Observe, he says, how little reality there
is in any speech about matters with which people are
not familiar, how absurdly a person entirely unfamiliar
with military affairs will blunder if he attempts to
make arrangements for the commissariat of an army,
or how many ridiculous mistakes will be made by a
foreigner who comes over and dashes at once into plans
for the supply of our markets. It would be like the
mistakes of a dim-sighted man in judging of colours,
or a person who had no knowledge of music in criticizing
a performance on the organ. It is the same when a
stranger offers an amiable panegyric on the manners
and character of some one of whom he knows nothing.
They praise the wrong things, and if they find fault
at all, imagine slights where no slight was intended,
discover imaginary meanings in events, and do not
understand the difference between one point and

[1] *Parochial and Plain Sermons*, vol. v., ser. iii. p. 33, edition
of 1868.

another. "They look at them as infants gaze at the objects which meet their eyes, in a vague, unapprehensive way, as if not knowing whether a thing is a hundred miles off or close at hand, whether great or small, hard or soft." [1] Just so unreal, he says, are most men in their religious duties. They pray not with all their hearts in their prayer, but are full of self-consciousness, and dwell on the solemnity of the act in which they are engaged, and attempt to rise to the occasion by feeding their mind on the thought of the greatness of God and the insignificance of man. That is not prayer, but only an inflated reverie to which the thought of prayer may give rise. Of this nature are the commonplaces about the vanity of life and the certainty of death, or the reflections to which people often give utterance in sickness or low spirits—"lifeless sounds whether of pipe or harp." The whole drift of the sermon is concentrated in the sentence, "Aim at *things*, and your words will be right without aiming." [2] "Let us avoid talking of whatever kind, whether mere empty talking, or censorious talking, or idle profession, or descanting upon Gospel doctrines, or the affectation of philosophy, or the pretence of eloquence." [3] I sincerely believe that *many* men's lives have been much sincerer and more genuine than they otherwise would have been for the writing and publication of this sermon.

But though reality was the first of Newman's characteristics as a preacher, it would not have been half as effective as it was, had it not been combined with that profound and vivid apprehension of the truth

[1] *Parochial and Plain Sermons*, vol. v., ser. iii. p. 36, edition of 1868.　　　[2] *Ibid.* p. 44.　　　[3] *Ibid.* p. 45.

and the marvel of revelation which is so seldom united with realism such as his. Sincere preachers have abounded in recent years, preachers who have shown their sincerity by openly discarding the belief in those truths of the Christian revelation which cannot, after some sort of fashion, be reconciled to what is called "modern thought." Newman held that modern thought needed reforming in the light of the Christian revelation, not the Christian revelation in the light of modern thought. Comparatively early in his pulpit at St. Mary's, as early as 26th August, 1832, he had denounced "the religion of the day," expressly because it accepted only that side of revealed religion which fell in with the tendencies of modern civilization, because it substituted enlightened prudence, or the love of the beautiful, or a mixture of the two, for the awe and fear which conscience inspires and Divine revelation sternly enforces. He did not accommodate his religion to the moral and intellectual atmosphere in which he found himself. If he had, it might have been comparatively easy to him to make men realize vividly what they were, and what he wished them to become. On the contrary, what he wished them to become, involved in every respect a very painful change of attitude, a change which they could not bring about without going through much inward tribulation. "I do not at all deny," he said, "that this spirit of the world uses words and makes professions which it would not adopt except for the suggestions of Scripture; nor do I deny that it takes a general colouring from Christianity, so as really to be modified by it, nay, in a measure, enlightened and exalted by it. Again, I fully grant that many persons in whom this bad spirit shows itself are but partially infected by it, and at bottom good Christians though imperfect. Still, after all here is an existing teaching only partially evangelical, built upon worldly principle, yet pretending to be the Gospel, dropping one whole side of the Gospel, its austere character, and considering it enough to be benevolent, courteous, candid, correct in conduct, delicate,—though it includes no true fear of God, no fervent zeal for His honour, no deep hatred of sin, no horror at the sight of sinners, no indignation and compassion at the blasphemies of heretics, no jealous adherence to doctrinal truth, no especial sensitiveness about the particular means of gaining ends, providing the ends be good, no loyalty to the Holy Apostolic Church of which the creed speaks, no sense of the authority of religion as external to the mind, in a word, no seriousness,—and therefore is neither hot nor cold, but (in Scripture language) *lukewarm.*" [1]

This was the sermon in which Newman boldly denounced the optimistic religions of the day as shallow and false, and expressed his belief that "it would be a gain to this country were it really more superstitious, more bigoted, more gloomy, more fierce in its religion than at present it shows itself to be. Not, of course, that I think the tempers of mind herein implied desirable, which would be an evident absurdity; but I think them infinitely more desirable and more promising than a heathen obduracy and a cold, self-sufficient, self-wise tranquillity." [2]   " Miserable," he said, " as were the superstitions of the dark ages, revolting as are the tortures now in use among the heathen of the

[1] *Parochial and Plain Sermons*, vol. i. pp. 313-14, edit. of 1868.
[2] *Ibid.* p. 320-21.

East, better, far better is it to torture one's body all one's days, and to make this life a hell upon earth, than to remain in a brief tranquillity here, till the pit at length opens under us, and awakens us to an eternal fruitless consciousness and remorse. Think of Christ's own words, 'What shall a man give in exchange for his soul?' Again He says, 'Fear Him who after He hath killed hath power to cast into hell; yea, I say unto you, fear Him.' Dare not to think that you have got to the bottom of your hearts; you do not know what evil lies there. How long and earnestly must you pray, how many years must you pass in careful obedience, before you have any right to lay aside sorrow, and to rejoice in the Lord?"[1]

From this it is evident that Newman did not hesitate to preach unsparingly what he held to be the austere and threatening side of Christianity. And it is rarely indeed that a man who dares to do this, confronts the facts of human life, and the petty manœuvres and little self-deceptions of the heart, with the exquisite insight and delicate, unexaggerating candour which Newman displayed. Those who preach an austere religion usually take refuge in generalities, laying on the dull colours in impressive masses, which excite the imagination without bringing home to the conscience the actual significance of moral cowardice and worldliness. Newman made no attempt to pile up horrors, but while he kept to the language of Scripture in speaking of what was most awful, he showed a profound and accurate knowledge of the frivolities and self-deceptions of men which gave the world the measure of his appreciation and his hatred of what is worst in men.

[1] *Parochial and Plain Sermons*, vol. i. p. 323.

That a man with so precise and delicate an insight into the subtle and intricate web of human motives should display so hearty an abhorrence of that tainted interior self which he so well understood, and should accept the severest judgments upon it as the very voice of Divine justice, appeared a remarkable vindication of that sternness of the Divine mind on which he insisted with so much vividness and force. That so sympathetic and musical a voice should cry aloud and spare not, was of itself a singular testimony to the forbearance of the Divine wrath, and to the searching fire of the Divine love.

For the tenderness and pathos in these sermons are at least as striking as their delicate realism and their uncompromising severity. There is a genuine marvel in the combination of so much sweetness and pity with so much sternness. We almost hear again the thrill of the subdued voice as we read those passages with which the sermons abound, where the overwhelming miracle of grace is delineated. For instance—"All the trouble which the world inflicts upon us, and which flesh cannot but feel,—sorrow, pain, care, bereavement, —these avail not to disturb the tranquillity and the intensity with which faith gazes upon the Divine Majesty. All the necessary exactness of our obedience, the anxiety about failing, the pain of self-denial, the watchfulness, the zeal, the self-chastisements which are required of us, as little interfere with this vision of faith as if they were practised by another, not by ourselves. We are two or three selves at once, in the wonderful structure of our minds, and can weep while we smile, and labour while we meditate."[1]

[1] *Parochial and Plain Sermons*, vol. iv. pp. 146-7, edition of 1868.

Or take the passage in one of the sermons on the Epiphany, in which Newman illustrates from ordinary human life that transitory gleam of earthly glory which Christ had in His infancy, when an angel announced His coming, Elizabeth saluted Him still unborn as her Lord, when the shepherds worshipped at the message they received from on high, and a star blazed above the humble roof under which He entered into our sorrows. "It often happens that when persons are in serious illnesses, and in delirium in consequence, or other disturbance of mind, they have some few minutes of respite in the midst of it, when they are even more than themselves, as if to show us what they really are, and to interpret for us what else would be dreary. And, again, some have thought that the minds of children have on them traces of something more than earthly, which fade away as life goes on, but are the promise of what is intended for them hereafter. And somewhat in this way, if we may dare compare ourselves with our gracious Lord, in a parallel though higher way, Christ descends to the shadows of this world, with the transitory tokens on Him of that future glory into which He could not enter till He had suffered. The star burned brightly over Him for a time, though it then faded away."[1]

But what was most pathetic in Newman's sermons at St. Mary's was not so much the tenderness of feeling which he combined with great severity of conscience,—though that was most pathetic,—as the perpetual and constant struggle he made to convince a world that was not at all disposed to be convinced on

[1] *Parochial and Plain Sermons,* vol. vii. pp. 80, 81.

that head, that Christianity is not compatible with that
eager and almost headlong immersion in external pursuits and practical cares which seems to be the special
temptation of the English genius and temperament.
Englishmen, so long, at all events, as they restrain
themselves within given rules of conduct, are visited by
no compunctions when they plunge into life and take
their fill, as it were, of its joys and griefs, its anxieties
and cares.   They have no wish at all to be "detached"
from this cheery and vehement fashion of living, no conviction even that they *ought* to be detached from it.

But Newman from the first date of his preaching in
St. Mary's strove to drive home to his hearers his own
profound conviction that such a life is not the Christian's
life at all, and he pressed this upon them, till at last he
was all but convinced that he could not press it on
them with any success from his Anglican position, and
must find some other Church in which he could, in
his own opinion, more consistently preach that some
degree of detachment of the heart from the joys and
cares of this life, and of steady increase in the degree of
this detachment, is essential to that growth in the love
of God upon which all religious and moral discipline is
intended to concentrate itself and in which it should
find its consummation.   He seems to have become
gradually persuaded that this ideal of life was the
opposite of the genuine Protestant ideal, and that the
reason why Protestant nations on the whole beat the
Roman Catholic nations in the race for predominance,
is precisely this, that they give their hearts to that
race, while the Roman Catholics, the more they are
filled with the spirit of their religion, the more detach
their hearts from the earthly struggle, and when they

are untrue to it, illustrate the saying that " the corruption
of the best is the worst."

I have shown how trenchant was Newman's de-
nunciation of the mere religion of civilization as early
as 1832, thirteen years before he abandoned the
Anglican Church. During the whole of that time
an impression was, I think, steadily growing, which
eventually assumed the force of a conviction, that
the theology of the *Via Media* would not hold water,
that the religion of the *Via Media* would never hold
its own without the aid of those witnesses to the
blessedness of worship which regular religious orders,
devoted even in this world to the life of adoration,
afford, and that Anglicanism aims too much at a compromise between different ideals of life, ever to sustain
heartily religious orders of this kind. I have shown
his feeling as to " the Religion of the Day " in 1832.
Let me take one of the sermons of 1836 (vol. iv.
sermon xx.), called " The Ventures of Faith," which
shows how this feeling, that even the Christian life
of the Anglican communion was not what it should
be, was growing upon him even then, though he was
far from feeling as yet any doubt at all as to the
Church to which he owed his loyalty and love. He
asks, how would Christians be greater losers (as they
ought to be of course) than any other men, supposing,
what is impossible, that Christ's promises were to fail ?
" What have we ventured for Christ ? " he asks ; " what
have we given to Him on a belief of His promise ? "—
namely, that if we forsake all for Christ, Christ will Himself reward us both in this life and the next. " The
Apostle said that he and his brethren would be of all
men the most miserable if the dead were not raised.

Can we in any degree apply this to ourselves? We
think, perhaps, at present we have some hope of heaven;
well, *this* we should lose, of course; but how should
we be worse off as to our *present* condition? A trader
who has embarked some property in a speculation
which fails, not only loses his prospect of gain, but
somewhat of his own which he ventured with the *hope*
of the gain. This is the question—What have *we*
ventured? I really fear, when we come to examine, it
will be found that there is nothing we resolve, nothing
we do, nothing we do not do, nothing we avoid, nothing
we choose, nothing we give up, nothing we pursue,
which we should not resolve, and do, and not do, and
avoid, and choose, and give up, and pursue, if Christ
had not died and heaven were not promised us. I
really fear that most men called Christians, whatever
they may profess, whatever they may think they feel,
whatever warmth and illumination and love they may
claim as their own, yet would go on almost as they do,
neither much better nor much worse, if they believed
Christianity to be a fable. When young they indulge
their lusts, or at least pursue the world's vanities; as
time goes on they get into a fair way of business or
other mode of making money; then they marry and
settle; and their interest coinciding with their duty,
they seem to be, and think themselves, respectable and
religious men; they grow attached to things as they
are; they begin to have a zeal against vice and error;
and they follow after peace with all men. Such conduct
indeed, as far as it goes, is right and praiseworthy.
Only I say it has not necessarily anything to do with
religion at all; there is nothing in it which is any proof
of the presence of religious principle in those who adopt

it; there is nothing they would not do still, though they had nothing to gain from it except what they gain from it now: they do gain something now, they do gratify their present wishes, they are quiet and orderly because it is their interest and taste to do so; but they *venture* nothing, they risk, they sacrifice, they abandon nothing, on the faith of Christ's word."

And then Newman went on to say that St. Barnabas, for instance, had a property in Cyprus which he gave up for the poor of Christ, and that he therefore did something that he would not have done unless the Gospel were true, and that if the Gospel could have turned out a fable, St. Barnabas would have made a great mistake. But which of us, he asks, does what St. Barnabas did—gives up the prospect of wealth or eminence in order to be nearer Christ, or puts off worldly comforts, or schools himself by inflicting on himself voluntary penances for his sins, or even in prospect of wealth honestly and heartily prays that he may never be rich, because he thinks that riches would alienate his heart from Christ? Yet if we do none of these things, we are not really shaping our whole earthly course by Christ's promises, and making our life quite other than it would have been but for those promises. Such was Newman's pathetic impatience with the apparent absence in the Anglican Church of anything like habitual renunciation of the world as early even as 1836. But the feeling certainly grew rapidly before he first began to entertain any doubt that he was in a true Church. In a sermon preached on the 3rd March, 1839, on "Endurance, the Christian's portion," he expresses most pathetically his belief, that Christians who live a perfectly serene and happy life have

I

forfeited by their unfaithfulness the promise made to
Christians of suffering in this world, which our Lord
and St. Paul, and indeed all the Apostles, gave, and that
their prosperity and good understanding with the world
are as much proof that they are not living in obedience
to the revealed truth, as the troubles and sufferings of
the Jews under the Mosaic dispensation were proof that
they (who had been promised prosperity if they did
obey God's law) were not living in obedience to that
truth.

He insists especially on the prosperity derived
from the alliance of the State with the Church, as
a kind of prosperity earned by unfaithfulness to the
Church's true interests. " If 'the present distress'
of which St. Paul speaks does not denote the ordinary
state of the Christian Church, the New Testament is
scarcely written for us, but must be remodelled before
it can be made apply. There are men of the world
in this day who are attempting to supersede the
precepts of Christ about almsgiving and the maintenance of the poor. We are accustomed to object that
they contravene Scripture. Again, we hear of men
drawing up a Church government for themselves, or
omitting Sacraments, or modifying doctrines. We say
they do not read Scripture rightly. They answer, perhaps, that Scripture commands or countenances many
things which are not binding on us eighteen hundred
years after. They consider that the management of the
poor, the form of the Church, the power of the State
over it, the nature of its faith, or the choice of its
ordinances, are not points on which we need rigidly
keep to Scripture; that times have changed. This is
what they say; and can we find fault with them if

we ourselves allow that the New Testament is a dead
letter in another most essential part of it ?   Is it
strange that they should think that the world may now
tyrannize over the Church, when we allow that the
Church may now indulge in the world ?   Surely they
do but make a fair bargain with us; both they and we
put aside Scripture, and then agree together—we to
live in ease, and they to rule.   We have taken the
world's pay, and must not grudge its yoke.   Independence surely is not the Church's privilege, unless hardship
is her portion.   Well, and perhaps affliction, hardship,
distress, ill-usage, evil report, are her portion, both
promised and bestowed, though at first sight they may
seem not to be.   What proof is there that temporal
happiness was the gift of the Law, which will not avail
for temporal adversity being that of the Gospel ? . . . You
will say perhaps that the Jewish promise was suspended
on a condition, the condition of obedience, and that the
Jews forfeited the reward because they did not merit it.
True; let it be so.   And what hinders, in like manner,
if Christians are in prosperity, not in adversity, that it
is because they too have forfeited the promise and
privilege of affliction by disobedience ? " [1]

The pathos of this self-accusation, that he and his
friends had forfeited the *privilege* of adversity which
Christ had promised, by disobedience, seems to me
perfectly unique.   Yet pathos of this kind runs like
a silver thread through the whole series of Oxford
sermons.   Obviously Newman was very restive under
the political conditions of the Establishment, not only
because he wanted to obtain a greater independence

[1] *Parochial and Plain Sermons*, vol. v. pp. 290—292, edition
of 1868.

for the Church than the political alliance with the State admitted, but also because he resented the comfort, the ease, the sleek serenity, the worldly consideration and influence over worldly people, to which the alliance with the State had brought our Anglican clergy. He believed that no Church which was full of the spirit of Christ could possibly be on such good terms with the spirit of the world.

This was the line of thought which led Newman to the position which he took up so decidedly in 1843, when he was already wavering in his allegiance to the Church of England, as to the true character of "The Apostolical Christian"; and the pathos of his faith and his self-distrust was never more powerfully expressed.

He preached on this subject early in February 1843, and it was obvious from this sermon whither his thoughts were leading him.[1] It is possible, he said, to draw out from the New Testament itself the typical character-istics of the Christian of the first age of the Church, only we had read the passages which describe him so often that we had lost the power of taking in their true meaning. The first of the characteristics of a "Bible Christian" was to be "without worldly ties or objects, to be living in this world but not for this world." St. Paul says, "Our conversation is in heaven;" and again, "Here we have no continuing city, but we seek one to come." And it is from heaven, St. Paul tells us, that he looks for Christ. This, said Newman, was the chief mark of the Christian of the early Church—that he was one who looked for Christ, "not for gain, or distinction, or power, or pleasure, or comfort." The affections were

[1] The sermon is the nineteenth of those in the volume on *Subjects of the Day* (edition of 1869).

to be set "on things above, not on things of the earth."
Hence *watching* was an especial mark of the Scripture
Christian. "What I say unto you, I say unto all,
Watch." And the primitive Christians kept the command. "They were continually in the Temple, praising
and blessing God." "These all continued with one
accord in prayer and supplication with the women."
Peter goes up to the housetop to pray at the sixth
hour. Paul and Silas pray and sing praises at midnight
in their prison. The Church of Tyre bring Paul on his
way out of the city, and kneel down on the shore and
pray. And the result of all this watching and prayer
is that the primitive Christians became "a simple,
innocent, grave, humble, patient, meek, and loving
body, without earthly advantages or worldly influence."

They unite their possessions and have them in
common, and are of one heart and one soul, and distribution is made by the Apostles to every man according as he has need. They take literally the exhortation
to have their treasure in heaven, and not one which
moth and dust can corrupt; they obey the injunction,
"Let your loins be girded about, and your lights burning;" and again, that implied in "how hardly shall they
that have riches enter into the kingdom of God." They
take literally the suggestion, "No man that warreth
entangleth himself with the affairs of this life; that he
may please him who hath chosen him to be a soldier."
"Love not the world, neither the things of the world,"
was the rule of their life. "Be ye not conformed to
this world, but be ye transformed by the renewing of
your mind," was the ideal of their inward character.
They earnestly desired with St. Paul that the world
should be crucified to them, and they unto the world.

In a word, "they love God, and give up the world." And finally, they glory in their tribulations, to use St. Paul's language. These troubles borne for Christ are a genuine source of joy to them. They are blessed in their mourning, and in their hungering and thirsting, and poverty and privations, as Christ promised them that they should be. Newman then entreats his hearers in the following pathetic words—" Bear to look at the Christianity of the Bible; bear to contemplate the idea of a Christian traced by inspiration without gloss or comment, or tradition of men. Bear to have read to you a number of texts, texts which might be multi-plied sevenfold; texts which can be confronted by no others; which are no partial selections, but a specimen of the whole of the New Testament." [1] It does not follow, he says, that all men are called upon to imitate this model to the life,—though he does not explain why it does not follow, supposing that these commands were given, as they were, to all the first disciples of Christ, and that apparently they were followed by the primitive Church as a whole;—but whether that follows or not, it is at least true that this was the life enjoined on His followers by our Lord, and it is also true, that in all ages there have been plenty of persons who followed them literally. When asked who these are, Newman answers, —and it must have taken great gallantry and courage to make this answer in an Oxford pulpit at that day,— " I am loth to say; I have reason to ask you to be honest and candid, for so it is, as if from consciousness of the fact, and dislike to have it urged upon us, we and our fore-fathers have been accustomed to scorn and ridicule these

[1] Newman's sermons on *Subjects of the Day*, edition of 1869, pp. 289, 290.

faithful, obedient persons, and in our Saviour's very words, ' to cast out their *name* as evil for the Son of man's sake.' But if the truth must be spoken, what are the humble monk and the holy nun, and other regulars, as they were called, but Christians after the very pattern given us in Scripture? What have they done but this—pepetuate in the world the Christianity of the Bible? Did our Saviour come on earth suddenly, as He will one day visit it, in whom would He see the features of the Christians whom He and His Apostles left behind them but in them? Who but these give up home and friends, and wealth and ease, good name and liberty of will, for the kingdom of heaven? Where shall we find the image of St. Paul, or St. Peter, or St. John, or of Mary the mother of Mark, or of Philip's daughters, but in those who, whether they remain in seclusion, or are sent over the earth, have calm faces, and most plaintive voices, and spare frames, and gentle manners, and hearts weaned from the world, and wills subdued; and for their meekness meet with insult, and for their purity with slander, and for their gravity with suspicion, and for their courage with cruelty; yet meet with Christ everywhere—Christ their all-sufficient, ever-lasting portion, to make up to them, both here and hereafter, all they suffer, all they dare, for His Name's sake?"

This is the sermon which seems to me to announce most clearly the change of faith which was coming, but which was still deferred for more than two years. And the pangs of the anticipated rupture give to the pathos of all his sermons at this time the most exquisite tenderness and depth. Evidently he had made up his mind that detachment from the world was

enjoined by our Lord on His followers, and could see
evidence of that detachment partially indeed in the
secular clergy of Catholic countries, but completely
only in the "Regular Clergy" of Christian monasticism.
He never explains why he thinks that which is obligatory on those who set the example, is not obligatory also
on the Christian community at large, why it should
need a distinct call to make it the duty of ordinary
Christians now, to act like the ordinary Christians of
the primitive Church. He suggests that Ananias and
Sapphira were not required to give up all their property,
but were only required to be honest in stating what it
was that they had given up. And he speaks of them as
a proof that "those great surrenders which Scripture
speaks of are not incumbent on all Christians. They
could not be voluntary," he says, "if they were duties;
they could not be meritorious if they were not voluntary."
But if that be so, surely a great part of the literalness he
has demanded for the interpretation of our Lord's words,
" He that loveth father or mother more than Me is not
worthy of Me ; and he that loveth son or daughter more
than Me is not worthy of Me," vanishes at once. Either
these and similar passages exclude from true discipleship
all who do not make these sacrifices, or they do not ;
and if they do not, surely they cannot be said to lay an
absolute obligation on the Church at all. However,
Newman had satisfied himself that what was imposed
on those who were to set a Christian example was not
inposed on all the followers of Christ, and this sermon
was the announcement that he could see no true Church
except where the ecclesiastical motive-power at least
was in the hands of men who had renounced the joys of
the world for Christ's sake, in other words, was in the

hands of a self-denying clergy, and under the moral influence of the great monastic orders.

Newman's next sermon, preached within a fortnight of this, and bringing out still more completely the deep pathos of his situation in a Church which he loved dearly but revered less every year, was that on "Wisdom and Innocence," which so painfully impressed the late Canon Kingsley, and served to convince him that not only had truth "never been a virtue with the Roman clergy," but that "Father Newman informs us that it had not, and on the whole ought not to be, that cunning is the weapon which Heaven has given to the saints wherewith to withstand the brute force of the wicked world, which marries and is given in marriage." And no doubt the sermon was Newman's own answer to the assertion that the independent ecclesiastical polity which he so much preferred to the humdrum Anglican establishment, has usually been disfigured by a diplomatic and furtive policy, which is plainly inconsistent with Christian rectitude and courage. What he said in answer to this was to put forward our Lord's injunction to His disciples, to meet the persecutions of the world of which He forewarned them by being "wise as serpents and harmless as doves." They were to go forth as "sheep in the midst of wolves," but not with the helplessness and witlessness of sheep. They were to injure no one, but they were to be prudent and wary, and not to expose themselves to unnecessary danger. They were to use a certain reserve, and not blurt out what would merely irritate the world without some sufficient hope of teaching the world. Now such conduct produces in the world the impression of duplicity and craft, an impression which is greatly heightened when it is observed

how successful Christians are in spreading their teaching not only in spite of their weakness but in consequence of it, for the blessing of God which rests upon
the diffusion of the truth, and has of course a supernatural effect, is not recognized by the world, and so
the world assumes that there must be great subtlety
and craft where there was really nothing more than
simplicity of purpose and the presence of mind which
absolute faith brings with it.   And no doubt Newman's
was a sufficient explanation of the disposition of the world
to ascribe craft and subtlety to the primitive Christians.

But Newman hardly recognized how thoroughly the
maxim that the corruption of the best is the worst,
applies to the ecclesiastical type of character, and how
often that reserve and prudence which Christ enjoined has been transformed in that character into the
duplicity and cunning which the world justly condemns.
"Bishops," he said, "have been called hypocritical in
submitting and yet opposing themselves to the civil
power in a matter of plain duty if a popular movement was the consequence; and then hypocritical again
if they did their best to repress it."[1]   No doubt they
have, sometimes unjustly, and sometimes quite justly.
It is a very difficult matter, especially when a great
and able ecclesiastic finds himself pitted against a
violent world, to keep his actions steadfastly within
the lines of strict Christian simplicity and charity, and
when he once transgresses these lines, he soon shows
us how much easier it is to discredit the Church than
to bring disgrace on the world.   I don't think that
the sermon itself was at all open to Mr. Kingsley's

---

[1] *Sermons on Subjects of the Day*, p. 306.

interpretation of it; but I do think that, considered
as an historical apology for the ecclesiastical type of
character, it did need much stronger admissions than
any which Newman gave as to the perversions to which
that type of character has shown itself to be liable. As
a defence of the humility and meekness of the primitive
Church, it is very effective to say, as Newman did of her
bitter enemies, "It is easy to insinuate, when men are
malevolent, that those who triumph through meekness
have affected the meekness to secure the triumph," but
men who were not malevolent have made that remark
concerning many of the ecclesiastical politicians for
whose indirectness of policy it was supposed—perhaps
mistakenly—that this sermon was intended to offer an
apology.   Perhaps the sermon would have answered
its purpose better if a franker confession had been
made, that Churchmen, in obeying their Lord's command, have been apt to mingle a good deal too much
of the wisdom of the serpent with a good deal too
little of the harmlessness of the dove; and that when
they have done so, they have evolved a type of character inferior instead of superior to the worldly character
which devotes itself to the same order of affairs.

On the whole, I think that Newman's extraordinary
power in the pulpit of St. Mary's was due to the
wonderful blending of the reality of his insight into
human life and character with his absolute faith in
revelation and the spiritual world which that revelation opened to his view, heightened as these great
gifts were by a nature singularly sensitive to the pangs
of lacerated feelings and wounded affections, and sub-
jected to a severe strain by his gradual discovery that
his ideal of the Christian character and Christian

doctrine was undermining his position as a Christian teacher, and demanding from him the one act of self-denial which he had long taught himself to regard as one of deliberate disobedience to the spiritual authority which he regarded as speaking to him with God's own voice. The great difference between his style as an Anglican teacher and his style as a Catholic teacher, was due to the profound pathos of his situation in the former position, and the comparative freedom of his situation in the latter. In both positions the delicacy and tenderness of his nature made themselves powerfully felt, but in the former he spoke like one repressing the anxious forebodings of his own heart, in the latter like one pouring out the pity of an enfranchised spirit.

As University preacher Newman perhaps hardly exerted so characteristic an influence as he did in the sermons in which he strove chiefly to drive home the significance of the Christian revelation. His University sermons may be said to be more or less attempts to discover the true relation of Reason to Faith, and great as these sermons are, abounding in passages of the highest power, and here and there of great eloquence, beauty, and pathos, they are not so saturated with the nature of the man, as the " parochial" sermons and the sermons on *Subjects of the Day*. Still the great series discussing the relation of Faith to Reason is a very memorable series, and the wonderful sermon on *The Theory of Development in Religious Doctrine* with which it closes, is probably among the noblest ever composed on what may be called the method of revelation. The whole series is full of new light on a subject which has been frequently treated since, the relation of implicit to

explicit reason, though seldom with anything like Newman's power and lucidity. Indeed, the subject interested
him so deeply that he took it up again five-and-twenty
years after his conversion in his *Grammar of Assent.*
Newman started with an exposition of the mistaken
idea which the sceptical world usually attaches to the
word "Faith," as a species of weak and superstitious
apology for reason, foundationless belief which contents
itself rather with an *excuse* for credulity than with
anything that deserves the name of evidence. A rustic
will sometimes adduce as evidence of some strange
event, that the tree under the shade of which it
happened is still to be seen growing, and that he
himself has seen it, or that the very room in which it
took place is known to him. Faith, according to Newman, is usually supposed by the world to be an imbecile
reason of such a kind as this. But in reality, he
argued, faith has its origin in eagerness to believe
that for which the evidence is more antecedent and
presumptive than *a posteriori* and inductive. But such
an eagerness to believe may be, and often is, a perfectly
just and in the highest sense reasonable eagerness,
where it is the outcome of the highest tendencies which
are implicit, or folded up in man's nature; whereas it is
an unjust and unreasonable eagerness to believe, where
it is the outcome of the poorer and baser part of his
nature; the difference being that in the former case
the eagerness to believe proceeds from what is supreme
over man, or divine, while in the latter case it proceeds
from what is selfish and tainted in man, and far from
having any authority to secure our submission. But
apart from the question of *moral* predisposition, Newman was concerned to show also how readily the

sceptical world itself does trust these prepossessions, which it regards as merely superstitions in the region of religion, when they are the prepossessions of a great practical genius, as, for example, a military genius like Napoleon's. "Consider," he said, "the preternatural sagacity with which a great general knows what his friends and enemies are about, and what will be the final result, and where, of their combined movements, and then say whether, if he were required to argue the matter in word or on paper, all his most brilliant conjectures might not be refuted, and all his producible reasons exposed as illogical."[1] In other words, such a general reasons by the antecedent presumptions of the case, and the least straw of evidence is sufficient to confirm these presumptions, whereas, if he had gone by the explicit evidence alone, he could not have ventured to draw any confident conclusions at all. Whence does such a general gather his antecedent presumptions? Evidently from all his previous studies, and partly even from all his previous reveries and imaginations as to the proper mode of conducting campaigns, just as a first-rate mountaineer, to use another of Newman's illustrations,[2] uses all his previous experience in climbing when he scales a steep cliff, using his eyes, his hands, his feet, his physical endowments of every kind, in some combination of which he cannot in the least analyze the proportions, and one probably which no one else could imitate, to achieve a feat which no one else could perform.

"And such is the way in which all men, gifted or not gifted, commonly reason—not by rule, but by an

[1] *University Sermons*, pp. 217, 218 ; 3rd edition, 1872.
[2] *Ibid.* p. 257.

inward faculty." Newman held that this especially
applies to the way in which faith outstrips what is
ordinarily called evidence. Just as a man who knows
another intimately will judge by the slightest grain of
evidence undecipherable to any one else what was his
motive and what his line of conduct under given circumstances, though the actual story of what he did
may be only half extant, so the prophet or apostle understood what God was doing before any one else understood it, and so the disciple of that prophet or
apostle understood what his Master intended when the
outside world was in perplexity and amazement. And
so too in all the moral experience of life, the quick and
vigilant conscience finds the clue to God's purposes
more easily and with more certainty than the slow and
sluggish conscience; and what one man rejects as
evidence altogether, and deems too trivial to be of any
account, except to the superstitious, and from his point
of view rightly so rejects, another man with a different
moral experience accepts eagerly as for him absolutely
convincing, and rightly so accepts. In short, Newman maintains that implicit reasoning is a far more
active and useful agent in actual life than explicit
reasoning, and accounts for a great deal more of the
practical wisdom of life. Courts of justice must go
chiefly by explicit evidence, as they are not familiar
with the ways and motives of those with whom they
deal; but it would be as foolish for men who do know
these ways and motives to trammel themselves with
legal rules, as it would for Marlborough or Napoleon
to trammel themselves with the formal principles of
strategy, though their own minds contained not only
all that had yielded these formal principles, but a great

deal more beside. And especially Newman maintains,
that in judging of revelation man must guide himself,
if he would guide himself rightly, more by the craving
and love for God, which is God's witness in the heart,
than by the external evidence of the supernatural as
it is presented to him in treatises on Christian evidence.

Newman took up the same theme in the great
University sermon on "The Theory of Development in
Religious Doctrine."   It was preached in February 1843,
and was, I suppose, the last University sermon preached
by him in the University pulpit, though he remained
an Anglican, nominally at least, during the two years
of his retirement at Littlemore. In that sermon he
starts virtually from the maxim which, as he tells us, he
learnt from Scott, the author of the commentaries, that
the true test of life is growth, but he applies it in
a somewhat novel way to the dogmatic development
of the impressions derived from revelation.   "Reason,"
he said, "has not only submitted, it has ministered to
faith ; it has illustrated its documents ; it has raised
illiterate peasants into philosophers and divines ; it has
elicited a meaning from their words which their immediate hearers little suspected. Stranger surely is it
that St. John should be a theologian than that St.
Peter should be a prince. This is a phenomenon proper
to the gospel and a note of divinity. Its half sentences,
its overflowings of language, admit of development ; they
have a life in them which shows itself in progress ; a
truth which has the token of consistency ; a reality
which is fruitful in resources ; a depth which extends
into mystery ; for they are representations of what is
actual, and has a definite location, and necessary bearing, and a meaning in the great system of things, and

a harmony in what it is, and a compatibility in what it involves. What form of Paganism can furnish a parallel? What philosopher has left his words to posterity as a talent which could be put to usury, as a mine which could be wrought? Here too is the badge of heresy; its dogmas are unfruitful; it has no theology, so far forth as it is heresy it has none. Deduct its remnant of Catholic theology and what remains? Polemics, explanations, protests." [1]

Newman goes on to explain the process by which the impressions of God derived from the inspired teachers of the Church took hold of the mind of the first ages and worked upon them—often without getting any explicit acknowledgment for years or even centuries together,— yet showing their vitality at least by the decision with which they rejected and shook off misconceptions inconsistent with their full development. "The Christian mind," he says, "reasons out a series of dogmatic statements one from another," but reasons them out "not from those statements taken in themselves as logical propositions, but as being itself enlightened and (as if) inhabited by that sacred impression which is prior to them, which acts as a regulating principle, ever present, upon the reasoning, and without which no one has any warrant to reason at all. Such sentences as 'the Word was God,' or as 'the Only-begotten Son who is in the bosom of the Father,' or 'the Word was made flesh,' or 'the Holy Ghost which proceedeth from the Father,' are not a mere letter which we may handle by the rules of art at our own will, but august tokens of most simple, ineffable, adorable facts, embraced, enshrined

[1] *University Sermons*, pp. 317, 318.

K

according to its measure in the believing mind."[1] Thus " Scripture begins a series of developments which it does not finish," but it records these first living impressions, while the developed dogmas do but mark out, as it were, so far as it is possible to do so, the real range, depth, and character of those impressions.

The multiplicity of propositions implies no multiplicity of dogmas, but resembles rather the multiplicity of observations taken in the trigonometrical survey of any country, of any conspicuous landmark or mountain-top. These imply, of course, no complexity in that landmark, but only that it is necessary to determine the bearing upon it of all the other points from which it can be seen.   Observations are added to observations not with the view of multiplying landmarks, but with the view of making it quite clear how other things stand with relation to it.   And so propositions are added to propositions in the definition of dogma, not because the Divine reality described is itself complex, but because being so much beyond and above us, it is not easy to fix our thoughts with regard to it without describing the impressions it makes upon us from a great many different points of view.

But then Newman raises the abstract difficulty, how it is possible for the infinite Being to make on a finite being any adequate impression that will reveal His nature at all.   If God's nature is infinite, the impression or idea it produces within us must be infinite also in order to be adequate; and if our nature is finite, no impression or idea to which it is adequate can be other than finite.   And to a certain extent Newman concedes

[1] *University Sermons*, p. 334.

this, since Scripture itself treats our human knowledge
even of God as He is revealed as necessarily inadequate,
as the knowledge obtained by gazing through a glass
darkly, and not as it will be when we are face to face;
but he maintains that though it may be inadequate,
it need not be without that real correspondence with
the Divine nature which constitutes real knowledge.
Just as geometry and the higher analysis are totally
different, and each in their way inadequate methods
of elaborating the same necessary truths, one failing to
cover the ground at one point, the other falling short
at another point, and yet both agreeing substantially in
their results, and each enabling us to push our real
knowledge of space further, so he says theology by
calling in symbol and metaphor, and making use now
of one part of our nature, now of another, by stimulating
our conscience, exalting the emotions, and stretching
our intellectual grasp, gives us knowledge of the
real correspondence between God's nature and ours.
And then he goes on to that noble passage, probably
unequalled in its kind since the writings of St.
Augustine, in which he dwells upon the wonders of
musical expression, as suggesting that in spite of its
limitations, human nature contains within itself elements capable of expansion into infinite and eternal
meanings :—" There are seven notes in the scale ;
make them fourteen, yet what a slender outfit for
so vast an enterprise ! What science brings so much
out of so little ? Out of what poor elements does
some great master in it create his new world !
Shall we say that all this exuberant inventiveness is
a mere ingenuity or trick of art, like some game or
fashion of the day, without reality, without meaning ?

We may do so, and then perhaps we shall also account
the science of theology to be a matter of words; yet as
there is a divinity in the theology of the Church,
which those who feel cannot communicate, so is there
also in the wonderful creation of sublimity and beauty
of which I am speaking. To many men the very names
which the science employs are utterly incomprehensible.
To speak of an idea or a subject seems to be fanciful
or trifling; to speak of the views which it opens upon
us to be childish extravagance; yet is it possible that
that inexhaustible evolution and disposition of notes,
so rich yet so simple, so intricate yet so regulated, so
various yet so majestic, should be a mere sound which
is gone and perishes? Can it be that these mysterious
stirrings of heart, and keen emotions, and strange
yearnings after we know not what, and awful impressions from we know not whence, should be wrought
in us by what is unsubstantial, and comes and goes,
and begins and ends in itself? It is not so; it cannot
be. No; they have escaped from some higher sphere;
they are the outpourings of eternal harmony in the
medium of created sound; they are echoes from our
Home; they are the voice of Angels, or the magnificat
of Saints, or the living laws of Divine government, or
the Divine Attributes; something are they beside
themselves, which we cannot compass, which we cannot
utter—though mortal man, and he perhaps not otherwise distinguished above his fellows, has the gift of
eliciting them." [1]

And then passing into that idealistic mood of
thought to which he had been prone from his earliest

[1] *University Sermons*, pp. 346-7, 3rd edition.

boyhood, Newman suggests once more that, knowing so little as we do of the ultimate causes even of our sensations and perceptions, it may well be that the whole structure of the universe, physical no less than intellectual and moral, is but a system intended to educate the spirit into a right frame of mind towards the moral and spiritual realities of the universe, indeed to inspire us with trust—trust that the knowledge which we gain from it, whether it be greater or less, whether it be exact or vague, whether it tell us precisely what we suppose it to tell us, or only brings our minds as closely as they admit of being brought into correspondence with the ultimate realities of things, is the best that we could have in our present state, and may be implicitly depended on to do for us all that knowledge could do until "the day break and the shadows flee away." In other words, if the theological conceptions provided by revelation are to be regarded as purely relative, and as adapted more or less to our finite apprehension, yet so far from there being any reason to think of them as less intrinsically true than the affirmations of our senses and our judgments concerning sensible objects, there is not a little reason to suppose that while all are relative to our capacities, these truths of revelation are those which approximate more closely to absolute truths than any others within our reach. The highest creeds are doubtless unworthy of the Divine verities, but they contain the fullest measure of truth of which our nature admits. They contain the truth "as far as they go, and under the conditions of thought which human feebleness imposes. It is true that God is without beginning, if eternity may worthily be considered to imply succession; in every place if He who is a Spirit can have relations with place. It is right to speak of His Being and Attributes, if He be not rather superessential; it is true to say that He is wise or powerful, if we may consider Him other than the most simple Unity. He is truly Three if He is truly One; He is truly One if the idea of Him falls under earthly number. He has a triple personality in the sense in which the Infinite can be understood to have Personality at all." [1]

And perhaps this is the place to say that I think Newman in his idealism emphasizes too much the unknowable aspect of the Divine nature. Surely he insists too much on the pure mysteries revealed to us, and too little on that wonderful character of God displayed in the gospels, which is the consummation of all the teaching of the law and the prophets, and which is hardly to be classed under conceptions, which either assert or deny *boundary* at all. Is there not something in man's character which simply ignores quantitative rules and measures? Does it add much to our conception of our Lord's human nature and life to speak of it as bounded or as not bounded by finite limitations? Is it not like attributing colour to a thought, or locality to an idea? However difficult it may be for us to understand the relation of the Eternal Father to the Eternal Son, and of both to the Eternal Spirit, and of all three Divine Persons to the One God, it is comparatively easy to understand that God, whether Father, Son, or Spirit, or the unity of the three, is manifested in Christ, and that, in the singular combination of His meekness and His austerity, His

---

[1] *University Sermons*, p. 356.

mercy and His wrath, His patience and His unyielding-
ness, His resolve to shed blessing on evil and good
alike, and His unshrinking recognition that nevertheless
there are those who transform their best blessings into
sentences of condemnation on themselves, we get a
glimpse which cannot deceive us of the true creative
spirit, a glimpse which is none the less true though we
are in apprehension limited, and He unlimited. It
seems to me that Newman might have insisted more
than he has done on the absolute character of the
moral and spiritual revelation given us in the life of
Christ; and that it is more because this revelation
cannot stand alone, without some clear glimpse of how
the same being can have been both God and man,
that what he insists on as the dogmatic doctrine of
the Trinity has come to be of the essence of revealed
truth.

No one who knows Newman's writings well can doubt
for a moment that from first to last the conviction that
all the true light of the world is to be found in revelation has dominated his thoughts. But I think he
has insisted a good deal more than he need have done
on the subordinate difficulties before which the human
mind reels, and a good deal less than he need on the
commanding truths, in the warmth of which the human
mind expands. Admit that there are economies, admit
that there are adaptations, admit that there are
symbolic elements in theology which are at best only
the nearest approximations to the truth of which finite
minds admit, yet surely there are clear rays of absolute
truth, which are more than "economies," more than
adaptations, more than symbols of reality, in the
character of our Lord. He was like the sunshine and

the rain in diffusing his mercy on the grateful and the
ungrateful alike, and in turning the other cheek, as
Providence in its wider administration of human affairs
so often seems to do, to him who has struck a passionate
blow at Divine goodness. But while Christ impersonated the large and serene benignity of the Divine
nature, which so steadily ignores ingratitude and even
insult where they proceed from men who have not yet
come to themselves, who have not realized that they
are dealing with an individual character so far above
their own that their ingratitude and insults carry no
sting at all, except so far as they show evil in themselves, yet He impersonated also the sternness and the
inexorability of God towards perverted consciences and
consummated sin. Surely in this power of diffusing the
sunshine and dew among the evil and the good alike,
of ignoring importunity and irritability and exacting-
ness and even torment with that calm magnanimity or
even compassion which our Lord not only enjoined in
the Sermon on the Mount, but personally exemplified
in the agonies of the Cross, and yet of combining with
all this supreme Majesty towards human folly and
pettiness and misdoing, a power of reproving weakness,
and branding wickedness, and exposing self-deception
such as only the inspirer of the conscience could wield,
we may justly say that we have a revelation of God
that is much more than a mere economical adaptation
to human weakness, and that may fitly be called an
unveiling to our eyes of absolute truth. I cannot help
thinking that Newman, though he always insisted on
the certainty of the communion between God and the
individual soul as the very starting-point of revelation,
has conceded too much to those who speak of God as only

presenting Himself to us through sign and symbol and mediate adaptations, and has hardly dwelt enough on those aspects of revelation in which we see the very majesty and the very holiness of His character without even a film to hide its splendour and its purity from our eyes.

CHAPTER VIII.

ADVANCING ESTRANGEMENTS—*TRACT* 90, AND THE
JERUSALEM BISHOPRIC.

LONG before 1841 Newman had found that the *Tracts for the Times* caused much alarm in the minds of steady Anglicans, indeed in some of those who were not in any sense of the word Low Churchmen. In 1838 the then Bishop of Oxford (Dr. Bagot) made some slight animadversion on their character which was more or less of the nature of censure. Newman offered to stop them at once if his Bishop wished it. But at that time the Bishop declined to express any such wish. The truth is, that Newman was at the head of a movement of which, as he afterwards recognized very frankly, he was by no means the master. It did not move as he had hoped that it would move; it had a law of its own, like a mass of snow or a flood once set in motion, which can be controlled only by the laws of gravitation and by the general conformation of the surface of the country over which it passes. The *Lectures on Anglican Difficulties*, published after Newman became a Roman Catholic, confessed this plainly; and in a more biographic form, though not, I think, the form which the Cardinal would have given to the "History of his

religious opinions," if he had written it after the tem-
porary estrangement between himself and the late
William George Ward was at an end, he reiterated the
confession in the autobiography. In the *Apologia*[1] he
says—"While my old and true friends were thus in
trouble about me, I suppose they felt not only anxiety,
but pain, to see that I was gradually surrendering myself
to the influence of others, who had not their own claims
upon me, younger men, and of a cast of mind uncon-
genial to my own. A new school of thought was rising,
as is usual in such movements, and was sweeping the
original party of the movement aside, and was taking
its place. The most prominent person in it was a man
of elegant genius, of classical mind, of rare talent in
literary composition—Mr. Oakeley."

The most prominent person in this new party was
certainly not Mr. Oakeley, who, accomplished and
scholarly as he was, was hardly a man to lead a phalanx
which, as Newman says, "cut into the original movement
at an angle, fell across its line of thought, and then set
about turning that line in its own direction," but a
much more vigorous thinker and much more trenchant
exponent of thought, William George Ward. In the
very charming and brilliant account of this remarkable
man's earlier career, which was published in 1889 by his
son, Wilfrid Ward, we get such a picture of him as we
have seldom had painted of a subordinate leader embarked in a great movement. Without any of Newman's
clinging affection for the English Church, and with very
little of his profound distrust of mere logic, Mr. Ward
exhibited a willingness to carry Church principles into

[1] p. 277, 1st edition.

action, and a certain hilarity in braving the dismay
which that willingness produced, that made him to a
very real extent a thorn in Newman's side, though Ward
was at the same time one of the most loyal and ardent
of Newman's followers. He was indeed in almost every
respect a difficult and restless disciple. He loved a
certain bareness, not to say nakedness, both of logic
and expression, which stand in very strong contrast to
Newman's carefully and delicately shaded studies of the
many modifying circumstances which tend to qualify
the principles he enunciated. Newman speaks of the
difficulty he found in dealing with persons who called on
him on purpose to "pump" him as to how he got over
this and the other difficulty in the Anglican position.
Of these inveterate pumpers Ward must have been much
the ablest and most indefatigable. He loved just those
things in the Roman Catholic tendencies of the movement from which Newman most sensitively shrank.
He seems to me to have loved best the most carnal
forms of the Roman Catholic devotions, just those which
repelled Newman, because they put in a broad popular
form what Newman could only endure when veiled in
an abstract principle. Ward heartily admired what I
have elsewhere called the "glare" of the continental
piety. To dwell on and even exaggerate the Roman
Catholic view of the infallibility of the Church was his
delight. The cultus of the saints was no trouble to him.
The stress laid upon the worship of the Virgin filled
him with exultation. He held "Justification by Faith'
to be almost a diabolic doctrine, and asked Mr. Oakeley
whether it was not true that Melancthon was less
"detestable" than most of the Reformers. To such
a disciple the *Via Media* was like a strait waistcoat.

And he delighted in asking Newman questions which were difficult to answer in any spirit loyal to that *Via Media* view of the Anglican position, and then in retailing far and wide the concessions to his own difficulties which he had obtained.

There was a singular *naïveté* about Mr. Ward, a glee in either giving or receiving a severe intellectual cudgelling, which rendered it almost impossible to take offence at his hard hitting. He was the most bland of logical swordsmen, and would smile as sweetly if his view were denounced as wicked, as he would when declaring the view of his opponent to be an utterly abominable though logical inference from premisses which no healthy conscience would ever have admitted. Far from loving, as Newman did, the sobriety of the English Church, and finding in its studious moderation a note of divinity, Ward loved all the ostensibilities, not to say the ostentations, of the Church of Rome, as it had developed itself in its war with the world, the haughty claim of its priesthood to override worldly dignities, the effusion and the fame of its saints, the multiplicity of its miracles, the pageantry of its pilgrimages, the pride of its humility, the military grandeur of its organization, and the calm defiance with which it treated the imputation of superstition and of ignorant credulity. No doubt he was one of the most exacting of the many followers of whom Newman repeats that they kept saying to him, " What will you make of the Articles ? " For the Articles not only specially excited Ward's doctrinal detestation of the Lutheran view of faith, but excited also that dislike of compromise, that profound contempt for judicious trimming, which was one of the most marked of his characteristics, and which

soon carried him far beyond Newman and his ultra-
montanism, when once they had joined the Roman
Catholic Church.

Newman declares with obvious truth in his *Apologia,*
that he himself did not share the apprehensions which
the question, " What will you make of the Articles ? "
implied. It was not in the least his own sense of
difficulty—as it usually had been—which led him to
deal with the Articles in the famous *Tract* 90 ; it was
rather " the restlessness actual and prospective of those
who neither liked the *Via Media,* nor my strong
judgment against Rome," and of these Ward was much
the most active and the most vivid. " I had been enjoined, I think by my Bishop, to keep these men straight,
and I wished so to do ; but their tangible difficulty was
subscription to the Articles; and thus the question of
the Articles came before me. It was thrown in our
teeth, ' How can you manage to sign the Articles ? They
are directly against Rome.' ' Against Rome !' I made
answer. ' What do you mean by Rome ? ' and then I
proceeded to make distinctions," [1] of which the upshot
was *Tract* 90, the tract which practically determined
that the goal of what Newman calls " The Providential
Movement of 1833," was not to be in a Branch Church.
Newman held (1) that the Articles were really drawn up
against the *political* supremacy of the Pope much more
than against the doctrines of the Church of Rome, and
he himself did not favour the supremacy of the Bishop
of Rome over foreign Churches. (2) He held that the
Articles were expressly intended by the Government of
the day which prepared them, to gain over the moderate

---

[1] *Apologia,* pp. 158-9.

Romanists, and that they were therefore intentionally
so drawn up that "their bark should prove worse than
their bite."[1]   And (3) he insisted that in recognizing
the doctrine of the Homilies as "godly and wholesome,"
and insisting on subscription to that proposition, they
virtually declared themselves Roman Catholic in spirit,
for they treat several of the Apocryphal books as in the
highest sense authoritative; they treat the Primitive
Church for nearly seven hundred years as quite pure;
they recognize six councils as allowed and received by
all Christians; they speak of the Bishops of the first
eight centuries as of good authority and credit with the
people; they speak of many of the Fathers as endowed
with the Holy Ghost; they quote from the Fathers the
teaching that the Lord's Supper is "the salve of immor-
tality, the sovereign preservative against death;" they
speak of the meat received in the Sacrament as an "invisible meat and a ghostly substance;" they speak of
Ordination and Matrimony as Sacraments, and expressly
say that there are other Sacraments besides Baptism
and the Lord's Supper; they speak of "alms-deeds" as
purging the soul from sin; they talk of fasting, used
with prayer, as of great efficacy with God.   All these
doctrines are then promulgated in a book, whose general
teaching is declared in the Articles to be godly and
wholesome, so that it is hardly possible that they were
really meant to effect a complete breach with Roman
Catholic doctrine.   And (4) Newman urged that when
the Articles were drawn up the Council of Trent was
not over, and its decrees were not promulgated, and
this showed that the Articles were not directed against

[1] *Apologia*, p. 163.

the Council of Trent, but against something else. Indeed the Homilies, which are the best commentaries on the Articles, being recommended to us by the Articles, teach us clearly enough what the object of the compilers of the Articles was, namely, to get rid of the popular corruptions practically sanctioned in the Church of Rome, though not for the most part supported by any dogmatic decrees. Again, (5) the Convocation of 1571 enjoined that nothing should be preached except what could be proved from the Old and New Testament, and what "the Catholic Fathers and ancient Bishops have collected from that very doctrine." Here is clear evidence, in Newman's opinion, that the Convocation which imposed the Articles was very jealous of any attempt to break with Catholic antiquity. No wonder that Newman believed that wherever the Articles are vague, and do not define what they mean, their vagueness was intentional, and was to be interpreted in the most comprehensive and not in the most narrow and exclusive sense.

But what Newman did not sufficiently consider was, that the Anglican Church, partly in consequence of its alliance with the State, and the consequent loss of individual energy, and partly in consequence of the temper of the people among whom it ministered, and their inclinations to distrust Rome both for its political and for its hierarchical tendencies, had become identified more and more in popular estimation with the Protestant aspects of its teaching, and less and less with the views dear to the moderate Romanizers, whom the ecclesiastical authors of the Articles had felt so anxious a desire to win. The prevalent impression certainly was that the Articles had effected a breach with Rome, and though

there was plenty of room for a sincere interpretation
of them in Newman's sense, there can be no doubt at
all that to the world at large that interpretation was
a shock and a surprise, and a clear evidence that the
aim of the Tractarians was gradually to reconcile the
two Churches, one of which had been often denounced
by the other as the true Antichrist. Ward at any rate
hailed *Tract* 90 not so much as explaining a legitimate
interpretation to be put on the Articles, still less as
explaining the true sense in which they were conceived
and imposed, but rather as finding for them a non-
natural sense indeed, but still a sense not at all *more*
non-natural than that which would have to be put on
many portions of the Prayer-book by anybody who
regarded the natural sense of the Articles as expressing
his real faith, and whose difficulty would therefore lie
in the straightforward and candid use of the liturgy of
the Church. Ward's view was, I think, the true one,
that either the Articles must be strained very hard
to reconcile them with the Prayer-book, or the Prayer-
book must be strained very hard to reconcile it with
the Articles, and that this being once admitted, Newman's arguments were sufficient to justify the choice
of the Articles as the more proper of the two documents to be furnished with a non-natural meaning.

There was, as I have shown, real ground for supposing that those who framed the Articles were not anxious
to offend the more moderate Romanists ; there was
no pretext for supposing that those who drew up the
Prayer-book were not genuinely opposed to the Puritan
theology ; so that if one of the two had to be wrested
from the meaning that plain men would naturally put
upon it, Ward saw every reason why it ought to be the

L

Articles and not the Prayer-book.   But Newman would
not so much as admit that the sense he preferred to
give to the Articles was a non-natural sense at all.   I
believe that he sincerely thought it the most natural
sense of which, all things considered, they admitted,
and was astonished and indignant at the outcry which
Tract 90 raised.   Ward must have kicked violently
against the naturalness of Newman's interpretation of
the Eleventh Article, "that we are justified by faith
only, is a most wholesome doctrine."   This meant, said
Newman, that we are justified by faith only as being
the only *internal* instrument of justification, but not that
Baptism is not necessary—as of course he held it to be
—as an external instrument of justification.   Nor does
the Article exclude even "works" as a means of justification, if these works are done under the prompting of
Divine influence, for it is Newman's very wholesome
doctrine that there are Divine influences at work all
over the world, amongst those who neither have received Baptism nor can be said to have faith in any
full sense, and that the works which are done in obedience to these sporadic Divine influences do dispose
men to receive that fuller grace which brings with it
a justifying faith.   "Such," he says, "were Cornelius's
alms, fasting and prayers, which led to his baptism;"
so that, according to Newman, the Eleventh Article
neither makes faith the sole instrument of justification
(but only the sole internal instrument), nor even the
sole internal instrument which *prepares* the way for
justification, since works done in deference to Divine
promptings prepare the way for the gift of justifying
faith.

All this diplomatic concession to the doctrine of

Justification by Faith, and elaborate limitation of it, was wormwood to Mr. Ward, and no doubt induced him to write a kind of defence of *Tract* 90, which was, in its tone, decidedly displeasing to Newman, who had no wish at all to see his view of the Articles treated as a mere *pis-aller*, excusable only because on any other view of them some still more weighty expression of the Church's faith must have been sacrificed. Still more questionable was Newman's mode of explaining away the Twenty-second Article on "Purgatory, Pardon, Images, Relics, and Invocation of Saints," so as to admit all these, though not in the form in which "the Romish doctrine" admits them. For example, Invocation of Saints is, Newman thinks, admissible, so long as it is not the kind of invocation proper to prayers addressed to God. I think this view would have been altogether over-strained and inadmissible if the Books of Homilies had not been sanctioned by the Articles; but as these Books—of which the English people virtually know nothing—do distinguish between invoking the aid of angels and saints, and giving them the sort of worship "due and proper unto God," Newman had a case for insisting on this distinction, though it must be admitted that the article on the subject, if it intended to allow that distinction, was one of the most misleading Articles of Religion ever devised.

On the whole, *Tract* 90 certainly gave a very false impression of Newman's mind and genius to the English people, and yet for a long time it was the one publication with which his name was chiefly associated. Oxford men indeed knew what he was as a preacher, and how deep as well as justly grounded was his spiritual influence over men. But for a long time the only conception of

Newman in the minds of the English middle-class was the conception of a subtle-minded ecclesiastical special pleader, who could explain away the force of the most unmistakable language, and show how to drive a coach-and-six through the accidental gaps in a Protestant formula. As a matter of fact, nothing less deeply characteristic of Newman than *Tract* 90 has ever been issued by him. It was very far indeed from an insincere document; it expressed, as I have said, what he thought to be the almost inevitable interpretation to be put on a far from straightforward ecclesiastical manifesto, looking to the time when it was drawn up, the persons on whose behalf it was put forth, and the Convocation by which it was promulgated. But though Newman really thought it the best interpretation of which the Articles admitted, that was only because, looked at from the historical point of view, they admitted of no very natural or straightforward interpretation at all. And it is never a very pleasant office for a man who is himself in passionate earnest, as Newman was, to take refuge behind the ambiguities of a creed artfully devised to suit the views of two very distinct parties, whose whole drift was at bottom irreconcilable. I have never quite understood how, with Newman's view of the Church, he was willing to belong to one which had gone so far in the direction of superficially at least disavowing doctrines which he himself was disposed to hold very sacred.

It is not necessary to describe what has been described hundreds of times—the storm of indignation which *Tract* 90 aroused. Newman, as he tells us in his *Apologia*, was quite unprepared for it, and startled by its violence, but his feeling on the whole was one

of relief that he was so distinctly pointed out as unfit
to retain any longer his place at the head of the movement.   He says in his *Apologia*, in relation to the
attack upon *Tract* 90, "I recognize" [in it] "much of
real religious feeling, much of honest and true principle,
much of straightforward, ignorant common-sense." But
his Oxford leadership was gone for ever. "It was
simply an impossibility that I could say anything
henceforth to good effect when I had been posted up
by the marshal on the buttery-hatch of every College
of my University, after the manner of discommoned
pastry-cooks; and when in every part of the country
and every class of society, through every organ and
occasion of opinion, in newspapers, in periodicals, at
meetings, in pulpits, at dinner-tables, in coffee-rooms,
in railway carriages, I was denounced as a traitor who
had laid his train, and was detected in the very act of
firing it against the time-honoured Establishment." [1]

But what affected Newman more profoundly than the
popular stir and indignation, was the evidence given in
episcopal charges, that the ecclesiastical leaders of his
Church utterly disowned the principles which attributed
to them so much higher a function as the channels of
Divine grace than was attributed to them by any other
Church party. "A bishop's lightest word *ex cathedrâ*
is heavy," he had written.   And an archbishop answered to the effect, that neither a bishop's lightest
word nor his gravest word is of any special account at
all. "Many persons look with considerable interest to
the declarations on such matters that from time to time
are put forth by bishops in their charges, or on other

[1] *Apologia*, p. 173.

occasions.   But on most of the points to which I have
been alluding, a bishop's declarations have no more
weight, except what they derive from his personal
character, than any anonymous pamphlet would have.
The points are mostly such as he has no official power
to decide, even in reference to his own diocese; and as
to legislation for the Church, or authoritative declarations on many of the most important matters, neither
any one bishop, nor all collectively, have any more right
of this kind than the ordinary magistrates have to take
on themselves the functions of Parliament." [1]

And how did the bishops' charges in general deal with
the Tracts ?   One of them replied in the words of the
Homily, " ' Let us diligently search the well of life, and
not run after the stinking puddles of tradition devised
by man's imagination.'   A second, 'It is a subject of
deep concern that any of our body should prepare men
of ardent feelings and warm imaginations for a return
to the Roman mass-book.'   And a third, 'Already are
the foundations of apostasy laid; if we once admit
another Gospel, Antichrist is at the door.   I am full
of fear : everything is at stake; there seems to be
something judicial in the rapid spread of these opinions.'
And a fourth, 'It is impossible not to remark upon the
subtle wile of the adversary; it has been signally and
unexpectedly exemplified in the present day by the
revival of errors which might have been supposed buried
for ever.'   And a fifth, 'Under the specious pretence
of deference to antiquity, and respect for primitive
models, the foundations of our Protestant Church are
undermined by men who dwell within her walls, and

---

[1] *Lectures on Anglican Difficulties*, p. 93, 1st edition.

those who sit in the Reformers' seat are traducing the Reformation.' 'Our glory is in jeopardy,' says a sixth. 'Why all this tenderness for the very centre and core of corruption?' asks a seventh. 'Among other marvels of the present day,' says an eighth, 'may be accounted the irreverent and unbecoming language applied to the chief promoters of the Reformation in this land. The quick and extensive propagation of opinions tending to exalt the claims of the Church and of the clergy can be no proof of their soundness.' 'Reunion with Rome has been rendered impossible,' says a ninth, 'yet I am not without hope that more cordial union may in time be effected among all Protestant Churches.' 'Most of the bishops,' says a tenth, 'have spoken in terms of disapproval of the *Tracts for the Times*, and I certainly believe the system to be most pernicious, and one which is calculated to produce the most lamentable schism in a Church already fearfully disunited.' 'Up to this moment,' says an eleventh, 'the movement is advancing under just the same pacific professions, and the same imputations are still cast upon all who in any way impede its progress. Even the English bishops who have officially expressed any disapprobation of the principles or proceedings of the party have not escaped such animadversions.' 'Tractarianism is the masterpiece of Satan,' says a twelfth."[1]

This was exactly the sort of testimony which Newman wanted to convince him that the life of the Anglican Church rejected the teaching of the Tracts, as every living organism will reject that which is alien to it, and inappropriate for its nourishment.

[1] *Lectures on Anglican Difficulties*, pp. 92-3.

Nothing seems to me a greater proof of Newman's sincerity and fidelity to his own intellectual convictions than the long period of hesitation through which he passed between 1841, when *Tract* 90 was condemned by the almost unanimous acclamation of the Anglican Church, and 1845, when he joined the Church of Rome. Even as early as 1837 he had received his first shock as to the tenability of the *Via Media*. In that year he was struck by the similarity between the position of the Monophysites of the fifth century—who denied the human nature in Christ, and who leaned on the Emperor, just as the Anglican Church leans on the State—and the Anglicans of our own time, who have so little of an independent doctrinal position, and who would have no popular strength at all if they did not receive help from their connection with the State, which always prefers a religious party that cannot stand alone, that is not stronger than itself, to a religious party which has so clear a doctrinal basis as to appear in no need of the sustaining power of the State. This impression Newman got rid of for a time, but it returned upon him after the outbreak against *Tract* 90. He had always ridiculed and denounced the notion of taking his stand on moderation alone. Before 1839 he took his stand upon antiquity. Between 1841 and 1845 he grounded his position on the impossibility of joining a Church which tolerated so many popular corruptions as that of Rome; but he never ceased to think and speak with scorn of those who balanced one admission against another without putting forward one clear principle, the men who held "that Scripture is the only authority, yet that the Church is to be deferred to; that faith only justifies, yet that it does not justify without works; that grace does not depend on the sacraments, yet is not given without them; that bishops are a Divine ordinance, yet those who have them not are in the same religious condition as those who have." "This," he said, "is your safe man, and the hope of the Church; this is what the Church is sure to want, not party men, but sensible, temperate, sober, well-judging persons, to guide it through the channel of no-meaning between the Scylla and Charybdis of Aye and No." [1]

For while Newman could rely on antiquity,—on his belief that the Roman Church had departed from the faith of the Apostles,—he was comparatively at ease in denouncing this meaningless moderation. But when he had convinced himself that Rome had only proceeded on the same principle in condemning those who denied the reality of Christ's human nature, on which she now proceeds in condemning the hesitating and half-and-half doctrine of the Anglican Church, he was no longer easy in his mind, and fell back on the negative position that it was impossible to join hands with a Church that tolerated so many popular frivolities, and that welcomed the aid of such unscrupulous controversialists. He said of Rome in 1840, " ' By their fruits ye shall know them.' . . . We see it attempting to gain converts among us by unreal representations of its doctrines, plausible statements, bold assertions, appeals to the weakness of human nature, to our fancies, our eccentricities, our fears, our frivolities, our false philosophies. We see its agents smiling, and nodding, and ducking to attract attention, as gipsies make up to truant boys, holding out tales for the nursery, and pretty pictures,

---

[1] *Apologia*, p. 193.

and gilt gingerbread, and physic concealed in jam, and sugar-plums for good children. . . . We English-men like manliness, openness, consistency, truth. Rome will never gain on us till she learns these virtues, and uses them; and then she may gain us, but it will be by ceasing to be what we now mean by Rome, by having a right, not to 'have dominion over our faith,' but to gain and possess our affections in the bonds of the Gospel. Till she ceases to be what she practically is, a union is impossible between her and England; but if she does reform (and who can presume to say that so large a part of Christendom never can?), then it will be our Church's duty at once to join in communion with the continental Churches, whatever politicians at home may say to it, and whatever steps the civil power may take in consequence." [1]

In July 1841 came the still-birth of a Bishopric of Jerusalem, the bishop to have jurisdiction over such other Protestant congregations as might desire to accept the bishop's authority, and this without any condition that such Protestants should renounce their errors and accept Baptism and Confirmation, where there was any doubt of their formal baptism. This seemed to Newman as decisive an admission that the Anglican Church did not insist on her Church principles, as the repudiation of *Tract* 90 had been that she did insist on her Protestant principles.

With reference to this matter, Newman says in the *Apologia*, "The Anglican Church might have the Apostolical succession, as had the Monophysites; but such acts as were in progress led me to the gravest

[1] *Apologia*, pp. 227-8.

suspicion, not that it would soon cease to be a Church, but that it had never been a Church all along." For the following four or five years Newman calls himself "upon his death-bed" as an Anglican. Like Heine's very different and much more penal sufferings in his *Mattrass-Gruft*, the experiences through which Newman went on his long death-bed certainly could not be said to constitute a euthanasia. He found many of his intimate friends very much disposed to take lightly the repudiation of the Tracts by all the chief authorities of the Church of England, and to go on much as before pleading the claims of the Church of England to the faith of baptized Anglicans on the old grounds. He himself could not do this. He regarded what had taken place as a virtual rejection of Church doctrines by the Church, and as practically confessing that the Anglican Church did not wish to be in communion with the Catholic Church. He accordingly fell back upon a new theory of his position—a new and weaker theory. He could not join the Church of Rome while it tolerated what he still thought such abuses as giving to the Virgin Mary and to the Saints a worship that he thought incompatible with the worship due to God, and therefore he held that he had no choice but to stay by the old Church in which he was born, and to justify that course as best he could. And the new defence was this. He observed that the Church of Israel from the time of Jeroboam was definitely excommunicated by the Church of the other two tribes, which remained the only Church of the true worship; but yet, in spite of this, two great prophets, Elijah and Elisha, were sent to this excommunicated Church, and moreover, the whole history assumes that Samaria was still under the Divine care, and that too without any condition being imposed on her people that they should submit to the Church whose worship was in the Temple of Jerusalem.

Under the awkward circumstances of the case, being unable to deny that his own Church strenuously repudiated what he thought the true principles of Catholicity, and yet unable to retreat to any Church that asserted them, Newman comforted himself by declaring that England was in truth in the position of Samaria, and that it was, the duty of true Anglicans to remain where they were, waiting for light, making the most of their Apostolical succession and their private right to cherish the doctrinal truth of which they had possessed themselves, in spite of the admission they were compelled to make, that their Church as a whole rejected that true doctrine.

This position Newman set forth in four sermons, preached in 1841, on the duty of remaining Anglicans under the great discouragement, as he held it to be, of the Jerusalem bishopric and the condemnation of *Tract* 90, Sermons 21 to 24 inclusive, of the volume on *Subjects of the Day*. They are amongst the most touching he ever preached, expressing with his usual pathos the pain of his position as a member of a Church whose mission appeared to have "failed," who "honoured not the precept of unity," who "had no heart for that outward glory of older times," but who, like Elijah fleeing to Horeb, the sacred mountain of the older covenant, "fled to Antiquity, and would not stop short of it," and "so heard the words of comfort which reconciled him to his work and to its issue." The comfort consisted in the assurance that after all, outward signs like tempest, and earthquake, and fire, even though the fire be the fire of cloven tongues such as descended at Pentecost, are not the final signs of God's presence, which is most truly discerned in a " still small voice," such as that which the prophet, even of a nation in apostasy, was permitted to hear.

Nothing could express more powerfully the mixture of anguish and of faith which filled Newman's heart at this time than the conclusion of the last of these sermons— " What want we then but faith in our Church ? With faith we can do everything ; without faith we can do nothing. If we have a secret misgiving about her all is lost ; we lose our nerve, our powers, our position, our hope. A cold despondency and sickness of mind, a niggardness and peevishness of spirit, a cowardice and a sluggishness envelop us, penetrate us, stifle us. Let it not be so with us ; let us be of good heart ; let us accept her as God's gift and our portion ; let us imitate him who, ' when he was by the bank of Jordan, . . . took the mantle of Elijah that fell from him, and smote the waters, and said, Where is the Lord God of Elijah ? ' She is like the mantle of Elijah, a relic from Him who is gone up on high."

Newman had thus already come to consider his Church a " relic " of older and better days. Evidently he had that secret misgiving about his Church which he here condemns, and it was a misgiving which grew upon him steadily. His resolve to remain in the Anglican Church was really hanging by a thread, though it hung by this thread for a considerable time, for even the *threads* of Newman's nature are very tenacious threads. In the four sermons from which I have just quoted he made it clear that in his belief Elijah and Elisha could only have acted as they did under explicit Divine instruction, —explicit instruction which he *assumes* but of course

could not prove to have been given,—and that it is only
right for men to remain in their original communion after
they have once been compelled to entertain doubts of
the grace vouchsafed to that communion, so long as they
are in serious doubt of the claim of any other Church
on their allegiance. So long as his conviction lasted
that the corruptions of Rome were too serious to admit
of his passing into her fold, he stayed in the communion
in which he was born—so long and no longer. But the
language which he had used against Rome was, as he
afterwards said, rather the language he had learned
from the Anglican divines of the seventeenth century
than the language which he himself had felt it his
personal duty to apply to her. When he retracted that
language in 1843, he declared that he had not been
speaking his own words, but had been following "almost
a consensus of the divines of my own Church;" and in
the *Apologia*—treating of these charges against Rome
and their retractation—he likened his position to that
of the convict who on the scaffold bit off his mother's
ear, on the ground that her indulgence of him as a child
had brought him to the scaffold at last. So Newman
accused the Fathers of the Church in which he was
born of having misled him into language against Rome
which, on thorough examination, he found himself unable
to justify, but which he had accepted in a filial spirit.
Apparently he felt disposed to bite off the ear of his
own Anglican mother for having taught him to revile
her whom he found to be worthy of all honour.

But while he was slowly finding this out in his retirement at Littlemore,—he had resigned his living at St.
Mary's on the 18th September, 1843,—he became the
object of unbridled curiosity, and the subject of an

unlimited number of rumours. "I cannot walk into or out of my house," he said, "but curious eyes are upon me. Why will you not let me die in peace? Wounded brutes creep into some hole to die in, and no one grudges it them. Let me alone; I shall not trouble you long. This was the keen, heavy feeling which pierced me, and I think these are the very words that I used to myself. I asked, in the words of a great motto, 'Ubi lapsus? quid feci?' One day when I entered my house I found a flight of undergraduates inside. Heads of Houses, as mounted patrols, walked their horses round those poor cottages; Doctors of Divinity dived into the hidden recesses of that private tenement uninvited, and drew domestic conclusions from what they saw there." [1]

In fact, the Bishop of Oxford (Dr. Bagot) was pelted with complaints that Newman was erecting an Anglo-Catholic monastery at Littlemore, and that the cells, chapel, dormitories belonging thereto were all advancing rapidly to completion. This was in 1842, before Newman had resigned the vicarage of St. Mary's. It was even alleged that Newman had already been received into the Catholic Church, and was founding a pseudo-Anglican monastery, which was really to be under the guidance of Rome; but this calumny the then Bishop of Oxford—a very excellent man—did not think it worth while even to repeat to Newman, in order that it might be contradicted. The charge that he was erecting an Anglo-Catholic monastery without even asking the consent of his bishop was mentioned, and was contradicted. Newman merely said that he was

[1] *Apologia*, p. 289.

building a parsonage for Littlemore, which it much
needed, without a chapel, by connecting together a few
cottages, and that for himself he intended to devote
himself more and more to religious meditation, though
not at the expense of the parish work, which he
zealously attended to; and that so far as regarded like-
minded friends, he was of course glad that they should
share his mode of life if they wished, but that no sort
of institution of any kind was in process of formation.
"I am attempting nothing ecclesiastical," he said, "but
something personal and private, and which can only
be made public, not private, by newspapers and letter-
writers, in which sense the most sacred and conscientious resolves and acts may certainly be made
the objects of an unmannerly and unfeeling curiosity."[1]

Newman was even accused of recommending those
who had already become Roman Catholics to retain
their preferment in the Church of England, and the
Bishop of Oxford was even misled into believing for a
time this accusation against him. This of course he
did not do, and indignantly resented the imputation
of doing, for he himself had set the example of resign-
ing his living long before he became a convinced
Roman Catholic. For more than two years after feeling something approaching to a belief that the Church
of Rome was the only Catholic Church of Christ,
though he still held it to be corrupted by a devotion
to the Virgin and the saints which amounted to a grave
unfaithfulness to the primitive teaching, Newman
remained in lay communion with the Anglican Church,
though he would not remain a clergyman of that

[1] *Apologia*, pp. 294-5.

Church, and this was the course which he also recommended to those who consulted him on such subjects. His own state of mind and feeling during these last two years of hesitation was very painful. One of his most intimate friends, an Anglican to the last, died in 1844, and he had expected, he says, that his death would have brought light to his mind as to what he ought to do. It did not. He wrote in his diary, "I sobbed bitterly over his coffin, to think that he left me still dark as to what the way of truth was, and what I ought to do in order to please God and fulfil His will."[1]

In such anxieties, hesitations, and doubts the period wore away during which Newman was on what he called his Anglican death-bed. There were many miserable searchings of heart, many seemingly unanswered prayers for more light, many slanders to be repelled, many unmerited but not unkind reproaches to be borne. And then at last the end came. The *Essay on Development*, of which I must speak next, written while Newman was nominally an Anglican, though substantially a Roman Catholic, was nearly finished, when in October, 1845, he felt that his conversion was really complete, and that he should imperil his salvation by remaining longer outside the communion of the Roman Catholic Church. But before I come to his reconciliation to Rome I must give some account of the remarkable essay with the composition of which his Anglican life terminated.

[1] *Apologia*, p. 359.

M

CHAPTER IX.

THE DEVELOPMENT OF CHRISTIAN DOCTRINE, AND RECONCILIATION TO ROME.

NEWMAN'S *Essay on the Development of Christian Doctrine* may be regarded either as the first of his Roman Catholic or as the last of his Anglican productions. In point of time it was the latter; in point of substance it was the former. Speaking of the last year of his life at Littlemore, he says, "All this time I was hard at my Essay on Doctrinal Development. As I advanced my view so cleared, that instead of speaking any more of 'the Roman Catholics,' I boldly called them Catholics. Before I got to the end I resolved to be received, and the book remains in the state in which it was then, unfinished." [1] Why the unfinished essay of which Newman thus speaks was never finished after he joined the Roman Catholic Church I have never been quite able to understand, unless it be that his fine sense of fitness discerned something appropriate in an abrupt termination to such a task, which he was unwilling to disturb. Although first published as the effort of one outside the Church to explain the apparent

[1] *Apologia*, p. 366.

changes which took place in the form of primitive Christianity, an effort which resulted in the writer's identification of that primitive Christianity with the Christianity of the Roman Church, there seems to be no reason at all, apart from reluctance to turn a tentative experiment in investigation into a formal demonstration, why the line of thought which was commenced while Newman was still in uncertainty as to its tendency, should not have been pursued and completed as a definite apology for the theology of the Church he has since joined. Of course he would have had to submit any book written by him as a Roman Catholic to the authorities of his Church, as he offered to do the *Essay on Development* in its present condition, —an offer which was refused,—but there is no ground at all for supposing that that necessity would have interfered substantially with the general drift of his argument. Even as it stands, the *Essay on Development* has, so far as I can hear, been adopted with enthusiasm by the most orthodox school in the Roman Catholic Church, and it is now usually regarded by Roman Catholics as one of the most powerful of modern apologies for their specific theological doctrines.

It is clear that what Newman was in search of, was a principle which should at once vindicate his life-long devotion to primitive Christianity, and yet discover in primitive Christianity signs of that capacity for growth which he had early learned from Scott, the commentator on the Bible, to regard as the true test of life. Primitive Christianity as a mere fossil, as a "deposit" which had to be kept apart from all the transforming change into which living principles blossom when they enter into combinations with so changeful and elastic

a universe as ours, and with a nature so full of all
sorts of potentialities as man's, had become nearly
inconceivable to Newman. He had begun to see that
even though principles remain the same, doctrines must
expand, must become explicit where they had been
only implicit, must assert themselves under new conditions which shed new light upon them, must explain
themselves, must illustrate themselves by giving birth
to moral consequences, to customs, to institutions, to
devotional forms; and that without such a developing
power as this, the primitive teaching, the deposit given
once for all, would be a dead formula, and not a living
power. The doctrine of the triune Deity must explain
itself. In what sense is God Three and yet One? The
doctrine of the Incarnation must explain itself. In
what sense was Christ both God and man? Was His
humanity real or only apparent? Was His personality
both human and Divine? or if Divine only, how was that
to be reconciled with a real humanity, if real it was?
Again, if sin is the fearful evil which primitive Christianity teaches it to be, what forces would be the most
suitable for stemming the torrent of this evil? To
what institutions should the penitent be submitted?
What are the emotions, and fears, and hopes with which
his weak nature may be legitimately aided to keep this
evil at a distance? And if the primitive revelation is to
be susceptible of this sort of moral development, what is
to be the check on this development? who is to prevent
it from so combining with the desires and hopes of our
nature as to degenerate from its former purity, and from
popularizing itself by virtue of that very degeneration?
Must there not be some guiding power which resists the
tendency of man's intellect, either to rationalize it, or

to cover it with parasitic superstitions, or perhaps to injure it in both ways at once? If Christ provided by the apostolate for authorities who represented Him when He had ascended into heaven, was it not probable that the Apostles had left behind them some successor to their authority, when they too, one by one, disappeared from the scene of their labours? Such were the questions which Newman set himself to answer in his *Essay on Development*, and the answers he found for them were answers full of devout subtlety, as well as answers in sympathy with the principle of what was to be the great scientific conception of the century.

When we consider that the *Essay on Development* was written in 1844 and 1845, many years before the scientific conception of biological evolution had been explained and illustrated by Darwin and Wallace, and a host of other writers, it appears to me that this essay, with its many admirable illustrations from biology, demonstrates that Newman's genius is not simply, as has been often asserted, a special gift for the vindication of authority in religion, and for the revivification of the past, since it betrays so deep an insight into the generating thoughts which are transforming the present and moulding the future. His discussion of the true tests of genuine development is marked by the keenest penetration into one of the most characteristic conceptions of modern science. Seven tests of a true development, as distinguished from a corruption, are given : (1) preservation of type, as the type of the child is preserved, though altered and strengthened in the man; (2) continuity of principles, in the sense in which the principle of one language favours compound words, while that of another does not; (3) the power of assimilating apparently foreign material, as a plant will grow luxuriantly in one *habitat* and only sparely in another, but assimilates more or less foreign material in any *habitat* in which it will grow at all; (4) "early anticipation" of the mature form, as the Russian nation began to aim at Constantinople centuries before they were a great power even on the Black Sea, and as Athanasius was made a bishop by his playfellows in anticipation of his genius for ecclesiastical government, or as Sir Walter Scott delighted his schoolfellows by relating stories to them when he was a mere child; (5) "logical sequence" of ideas, as when Jeroboam, in his anxiety to prevent a return of the ten tribes to their old allegiance, set up a worship that might wean them from their attachment to Jerusalem, on the express ground that if he did not, their religious instinct would be taking them back to their great Temple; (6) "preservative additions," such, for instance, as Courts of Justice, to the authority of government, which strengthen the government by protecting the obedient and punishing the rebellious; and finally, (7) "chronic continuance," as the chronic continuance of the American Union shows that the republican principle is still alive, whereas the gradual engrafting of imperial institutions on Republican forms, showed that the Republican principle was dying out in ancient Rome.

All these tests of true, as distinguished from corrupt or deteriorating, development are discussed by Newman with admirable subtlety, and a very fine sense for the scientific character of the conception of evolution itself, which would not be remarkable now, but was certainly very remarkable in the year 1845. He illustrates his first test—"preservation of type or idea"—by collecting the descriptions given of Christianity in the first three centuries by independent observers, and putting it to his readers what form of Christianity it is that now most closely corresponds to the type so described.   He gives the account of Tacitus, of Suetonius, of Pliny, shows how all these writers describe Christianity as something subversive of both political and social peace, as of the nature of a secret conspiracy, as possessed by a spirit of obstinacy, as insisting on the duty of addressing to Christ a certain form of words (carmen), and as even more mischievous and contagious through the inflexible resistance it inspired to any State decree which interfered with its rites, than through the morality it enforced, which is described as intrinsically unobjectionable, though tending to the break-up of the structure of human society as it was then understood by these writers.   He runs through the story of the divisions in the early Church, the Arian and semi-Arian, the Nestorian and Monophysite controversies, and shows how these divisions were caused by thinkers who rebelled against mystery in theology, and tried to simplify the truth handed down ; how, after the emperors became Christian, the heresiarchs almost uniformly sought, and often—like Arius, the semi-Arians and the Monophysites—found, help from the State, which naturally disliked the dogmatic independence and tenacity of the Church; and how it became almost one of the chief indications of heresy to lean on the civil power instead of on the doctrinal tradition of the Fathers.   And then he asks if there is no Church in modern times which excites the suspicion and jealousy of the world and the State, just as the Church of the first six centuries excited it, and yet stands alone and

unawed when it finds the powers of this world ranged
against it. Newman's conclusions are stated in a few
pithy paragraphs, first as to the Church of the first
three centuries, next as to the Church of the fourth
century, finally as to the Church of the fifth and sixth
centuries, and as they show the drift of his thought
very clearly, these conclusions I must quote. In sum-
ming up his review of the first three centuries he says—

"If there is a form of Christianity now in the world
which is accused of gross superstition, of borrowing its
rites and customs from the heathen, and of ascribing
to forms and ceremonies an occult virtue;—a religion
which is considered to burden and enslave the mind
by its requisitions, to address itself to the weak-minded
and ignorant, to be supported by sophistry and impos-
ture, and to contradict reason and exalt mere irrational
faith;—a religion which impresses on the serious mind
very distressing views of the guilt and consequences
of sin, sets upon the minute acts of the day, one by
one, their definite value for praise or blame, and thus
casts a grave shadow over the future;—a religion which
holds up to admiration the surrender of wealth, and
disables serious persons from enjoying it if they would;—
a religion, the doctrines of which, be they good or bad,
are to the generality of men unknown; which is considered to bear on its very surface signs of folly and
falsehood so distinct that a glance suffices to judge of it,
and careful examination is preposterous; which is felt
to be so simply bad that it may be calumniated at
hazard and at pleasure, it being nothing but absurdity
to stand upon the accurate distribution of its guilt
among its particular acts, or painfully to determine how
far this or that story is literally true, what must be

allowed in candour, or what is improbable, what cuts two ways, or what is not proved, or what may be plausibly defended;—a religion such that men look at a convert to it with a feeling which no other sect raises except Judaism, Socialism, or Mormonism, with curiosity, suspicion, fear, disgust, as the case may be, as if something strange had befallen him, as if he had had an initiation into a mystery, and had come into communion with dreadful influences, as if he were now one of a confederacy which claimed him, attested him, stripped him of his personality, reduced him to a mere organ or instrument of a whole;—a religion which men hate as proselytizing, anti-social, revolutionary, as dividing families, separating chief friends, corrupting the maxims of government, making a mock at law, dissolving the empire, the enemy of human nature, and ' a conspirator against its rights and privileges';—a religion which they consider the champion and instrument of darkness, and a pollution calling down upon the land the anger of heaven;—a religion which they associate with intrigue and conspiracy, which they speak about in whispers, which they detect by anticipation in whatever goes wrong, and to which they impute whatever is unaccountable;—a religion the very name of which they cast out as evil, and use simply as a bad epithet, and which from the impulse of self-preservation they would persecute if they could;—if there be such a religion now in the world, it is not unlike Christianity as that same world viewed it when first it came forth from its Divine Author." [1]

It is worth notice, perhaps, that in this passage

[1] *Essay on Development*, pp. 240-2, 1st edition. James Toovey.

Newman makes the suspicion, distrust, and almost
disgust with which what he regards as the true
Christianity was viewed, to be one of the main "notes"
of the Church; and that if that be so, the better Roman
Catholics are treated, the less conspicuous, according
to this passage, will be the "note" of authenticity in
the Roman Catholic Church. In a world which humbles
itself before such men as Father Damien, the apostle
and martyr who gave up his life for the lepers of the
Sandwich Islands, this "note" of the Church on which
Newman insists so emphatically can hardly be called
conspicuous.

After his review of the Church of the fourth century
Newman concludes, "On the whole, then, we have
reason to say that if there be a form of Christianity at
this day distinguished for its careful organization and
its consequent power; if it is spread over the world;
if it is conspicuous for zealous maintenance of its own
creed; if it is intolerant towards what it considers error;
if it is engaged in ceaseless war with all other bodies
called Christian; if it, and it alone, is called 'Catholic'
by the world, nay, by these very bodies, and if it makes
much of the title; if it names them heretics, and warns
them of coming woe, and calls on them, one by one,
to come over to itself, overlooking every other tie;
and if they, on the other hand, call it seducer, harlot,
apostate, Antichrist, devil; if, however they differ one
with another, they consider it their common enemy;
if they strive to unite together against it, and cannot;
if they are but local; if they continually subdivide, and
it remains one; if they fall one after another, and make
way for new sects, and it remains the same; such a
form of religion is not unlike the Christianity of the

Nicene era." [1] There again I should say that the
Roman Catholic Church of Pio Nono is much better
described than the Roman Catholic Church of Leo XIII.
Neither does the Church of Leo XIII. denounce external
heresy with anything like the same verve as the Church
of Pio Nono ; nor do the Christian Churches outside the
pale of the Papal Church denounce the Papal Church
with anything like the same vivacity. Indeed, there
is something like an *entente cordiale* between the Roman
Catholic Church of to-day and various other Churches—
an alliance against scepticism.

After Newman's review of the fifth and sixth centuries, in which the Nestorian and Monophysite heresies
flourished, he concludes thus—" If, then, there is now
a form of Christianity such that it extends throughout
the world, though with varying measures of prominence
or prosperity in separate places; that it lies under the
power of sovereigns and magistrates, in different ways
alien to its faith; that flourishing nations and great
empires, professing or tolerating the Christian name,
lie over against it as antagonists; that schools of
philosophy and learning are supporting theories or
following out conclusions hostile to it, and establishing
an exegetical system subversive of its Scriptures; that
it has lost whole Churches by schism, and is now
opposed by powerful communions once part of itself;
that it has been altogether or almost driven from some
countries; that in others its line of teachers is overlaid,
its flocks oppressed, its churches occupied, its property
held by what may be called a duplicate succession;
that in others its members are degenerate and corrupt,

---

[1] *Essay on Development*, p. 269.

and surpassed in conscientiousness and in virtue, as in gifts of intellect, by the very heretics whom it condemns; that heresies are rife and bishops negligent within its own pale; and that amid its disorders and fears there is but one Voice for whose decisions its people wait with trust, one Name and one See to which they look with hope, and that name Peter, and that see Rome;—such a religion is not unlike the Christianity of the fifth and sixth centuries." [1]

Is not that almost equivalent to making partial and local degeneracy of the Church, when it occurs without derogating from the authority of the Central See, one of the "notes" of the Church? Is it not almost equivalent to ratifying the judgment of that German monk in the Lutheran period, who was said to have been converted from his doubts by a visit to Rome, *because* he found the Church of Rome so corrupt and yet so powerful; his view being that no Church *not* divinely sustained could survive such corruptions? No doubt our Lord distinctly anticipates unfaithful stewards in His Church, but He certainly does not speak of them as being, even involuntarily, witnesses to the truth He had revealed. Such is the mode in which Newman deals with his first and chief test of a true development, the " preservation of type or idea."

In dealing with the second test of a true development, the continuity of the principles under which the development proceeds, Newman illustrates that continuity first by the resolute adhesion of the early and the later Church alike to the mystical as distinguished from the exclusively literal interpretation

---

[1] *Essay on Development*, pp. 316, 317.

of Scripture; and next by the resolute assertion of the early and the later Church alike, that faith is a better attitude of mind than doubt; that the highest mind inclines to take on trust what lower minds challenge till they have an adequate proof that their trust is legitimate—in a word, that the philosophy which (like Locke's in modern times) insisted on what is called evidence that a revelation was Divine, before reposing any trust in it, was the kind of philosophy which would have undermined all the greatest spiritual movements that the world has ever experienced, and extinguished all noble enthusiasm in the very moment of its birth.

As regards the first of these illustrations, the inclination to connect a mystical with a literal interpretation of Scripture, often attaching more importance to the mystical than to the literal interpretation, Newman shows that very early in the history of the Church Irenæus treats the account of the Annunciation to the Virgin Mary as in some sense a fulfilment of the prophecy in Genesis concerning the seed of the woman bruising the serpent's head, and argues for the dignity of the Virgin Mary as a nobler Eve, on the strength of that mystical fulfilment of prophecy. From Polycarp to St. Alfonso Liguori, according to Newman, the Church has steadily insisted on attaching the greatest possible importance to the mystical interpretations of Scripture. I do not suppose that any one who really enters at all into the spirit of Scripture ventures to deny the obviously mystical signification of many passages, nor the double current of meaning in others. It is hardly possible not to see the connection between the willingness of Abraham to give up his son to death on Mount Moriah, and the willingness of the Father to give up

His Son to death on Mount Calvary, though the one sacrifice was not completed, while the other was. It is hardly possible not to assign a prophetic and mystical meaning to Isaiah's prophecy as to the Son who should be called "Wonderful, Counsellor, the Mighty God." It is hardly possible not to regard such a psalm as the 104th, when it speaks of God sending forth His Spirit,—after He had withdrawn it,—" to renew the face of the earth," as an inspired anticipation of the sending forth of the Spirit on the day of Pentecost to renew the earthly life of man. But many of the mystical interpretations of the Fathers are altogether different, and seem to be even distinct perversions of Scripture. For example, Isaiah's prophecy as to a child not yet born, before whose maturity the lands of Syria and Israel should be forsaken, appears to admit of no double current of meaning at all. The date is fixed at which it is to be fulfilled, and that an early date; and the event prophesied is not of a kind admitting of a larger fulfilment in the future. Of course the reason for giving the passage a mystical interpretation was the apparent prediction of a supernatural birth, though that is a point on which the best modern Hebrew scholars are very doubtful; and as no supernatural birth is even alleged to have taken place within the limits of time assigned, the pious imagination identified the prediction with the supernatural birth of the Saviour of the world. That, however, is quite illegitimate while the strict limit of time exists, and cannot be explained away. The child's birth was to be a sign of the judgment coming upon Israel and Syria, and that judgment was to be fulfilled before he could choose for himself between good and evil. If the sign is to be disconnected with

the conquest of Syria and Israel, the prophecy as a prophecy disappears. Yet the supernatural birth (if the
Hebrew word indicates a supernatural birth) cannot
be pushed forward many centuries without disconnect-
ing the sign from the event which was to follow it.
Mystical interpretation in the sense of catching eagerly
at one single word in a sentence, and ignoring the whole
drift of the sense, is surely not so much mystical as
perverse. The objections reasonably urged against
such interpretations are not really objections to recognizing one event as a sign of another and greater event
of the same type, but objections to the practice of
subordinating the plain sense of an explicit statement
to the desire to discover a supernatural meaning, which
can only be squeezed into the language by a *tour de
force*. Religious mystery is not enhanced, but brought
into disrepute in the estimation of men, by the habit
of discovering it where it is not, as freely as where it is.

In relation to his second illustration of the test of continuity of the principle of development, Newman has
no difficulty in showing that the early Church and the
mediæval Church were equally eager to encourage that
forwardness to believe which springs rather from the
liveliness of the affections when the grace of God
touches them, than from reasoning. The New Testament is full of the censure of the unbelieving spirit, and
later theologians, like St. Thomas Aquinas and Suarez,
confirm its teaching. The real difficulty, I imagine, is
to distinguish between superstitious readiness to believe
and generous readiness to believe—the readiness which,
like Louis XI.'s, arose from selfish fear, and the readiness
which, like St. Francis of Assisi's, arose from generous
hope.

Then Newman goes on to show how the second test
of sound development—the continuity of the principles
by which development is regulated—blends with the
third test, the power to assimilate and transform alien
material, till the new life imparted to that alien material
brings about a complete transformation in the characteristic influence which that foreign material is made
the medium of diffusing. Sacraments of evil are
exchanged for sacraments of grace, and the very same
class of rites and practices which under a false religion
had degraded men, under a true religion purifies and
exalts them. Here he approaches, of course, the most
disputable of the positions of the Roman Catholic
Church, which has avowedly adopted the pagan ex-
ternality of ceremony with a freedom and a readiness
that has justified the suspicion with which it is viewed
as a compromise with superstition rather than a triumph
over it. Thus, as Newman quotes from the life of St.
Gregory of Nyssa, that saint "increased the devotion
of the people everywhere by instituting festive meetings
in honour of those who had fought for the faith. The
bodies of the martyrs were distributed in different
places, and the people assembled and made merry, as
the years came round, holding festival in their honour.
This indeed was a proof of his great wisdom, ... for
perceiving that the childish and untrained populace
were retained in their idolatrous error by sensual
indulgences, in order that what was of first importance
should at any rate be secured to them,—viz. that they
should look to God in place of their vain rites,—he
allowed them to be merry, and solace themselves at the
monuments of the holy Martyrs, as if their behaviour
would in time undergo a spontaneous change into greater

seriousness and strictness, and faith would lead them to it; which has actually been the happy issue in that population, all sensual gratification having turned into a spiritual form of rejoicing." [1] In one of his Roman Catholic books Newman returned to this subject again, and somewhat developed his view that Christianity had assimilated pagan practices, and turned them from sacraments of evil into sacraments of good. He admitted that besides exerting a spiritual influence on the men of good will, these transformed sacraments, which were originally concessions to childishness of mind, often familiarize the evil-minded with sacred objects and associations, which they learn to treat almost with contempt, though, as he maintained, without any abatement of their faith in the Divine power of the religion they thus ignore. The character of all these popular external observances of religion is, he declared, "pretty much the same as St. Jerome and St. Gregory Nyssen bear witness in the first age of the Church. It is a mixed multitude, some most holy, perhaps even saints; others penitent sinners; but others, again, a mixture of pilgrim and beggar, or pilgrim and robber, or half-gipsy, or three-quarters boon companion, or at least with nothing saintly and little religious about them. They will let you wash their feet and serve them at table, and the hosts have more merit for their ministry than the guests for their weariness. Yet one and all, saints and sinners, have faith in things invisible, which each uses in his own way." [2]

Newman's apology for all this mixture of careless or

[1] *Essay on Development,* 1st edition, chapter vi. section 2, pp. 358-9.

[2] *Lectures on Anglican Difficulties,* 2nd edition, lecture ix. pp. 231-2.

N

even deliberate evil with faith, is, that even if the faith
aggravates the responsibility for the evil, which I
assume that he would admit, though he does not say so,
it leaves the way open to a much less embarrassed path
of repentance than is available for evil done in unbelief.
He holds that it is not the *general* tendency of moral
evil in Roman Catholic countries to disturb faith.   The
faith remains through even many of the worst stages of
corruption of the will, and he thinks this a preferable
state of mind for the mass of men, to the unbelief into
which moral evil almost always plunges a Protestant.
But by the necessity of the case it is not possible to
show that this power of assimilation, in the sense of
a half-compromise with pagan rites, was ever really exhibited and sanctioned in the earliest age of the Church;
nor even, I think, that in the apostolic age faith was
thus retained in its vividness, in separation from
holiness and love.   That the Church showed great
power of assimilating pagan habits of thought, and of
leavening them more or less—often rather less than
more—with her own higher purposes, is obvious enough ;
but whether that did not involve a kind of toleration
of what is unholy, which the Apostolic Church would
have thought most reprehensible, is extremely doubtful.
I can hardly conceive an Apostle acquiescing in Newman's vivid presentation of supernaturally-minded but
pagan-hearted believers, as he afterwards gave it in his
lecture on " The religious character of Catholic countries
no prejudice to the sanctity of the Church."   I should
have thought that Christ not only taught that " If any
man will do His will, he shall know of the doctrine
whether it be of God or whether I speak of myself;"
but also implied the converse—namely, " If any man

will not do His will, he shall cease to know of the doctrine whether it be of God or not." At all events, I cannot help thinking that the state of a population absolutely believing in sacred truths which they openly disregard, is even more morally hopeless than that of a population which has gradually lost faith in the truths it has practically ignored.

Newman's fourth test of a sound development is the "early anticipation" of characteristics not fully developed till much later; just as we find in great men's childish character an early anticipation of their most striking mature characteristics. Goethe, for instance, often displayed as a child that deep sense of personal dignity and of something like authority which was so characteristic of his maturity and old age ; and Sir Walter Scott as a child used to delight his schoolfellows by telling them stories of his own invention, just as thirty years later he delighted the whole world. Just so Newman shows that in the first age of the Church there is the most remarkable evidence of that conception so fully developed and so elaborately applied in the Catholic Church in later centuries, which treats material things as susceptible of being made the channels of Divine grace. We are specially taught that the body as such, far from being evil, was like the whole material creation, a Divine work and "very good," that the Gnostic dislike to admit that Christ had come "in the flesh" was a fatal heresy—"Every spirit that confesseth not that Christ Jesus is come in the flesh is the spirit of Antichrist." As a consequence, even the mere earthly remains of good men were treated with a spirit the very opposite of pagan shrinking—with a passionate reverence and belief in their sanctifying influences. The very wood of the cross on which Christ suffered was regarded as full of virtue. And the feeling for relics, for sacraments, and indeed for all the physical objects which the Church consecrates, a feeling which Protestants regard as superstitious, was, in Newman's belief, a mere development of these early indications of respect for the material channels of Divine grace. Newman treats the cultus of the Virgin Mary as only one of the most remarkable developments of this creed, of which we have the anticipation in the account of the Annunciation, and of the visit of Mary to Elizabeth, in the early chapters of Luke's gospel. Another illustration of the early anticipation of a form of Church activity which assumed its fullest development centuries later, is the systematic and almost scientific treatment of theology to be found in the Ignatian epistles at the opening of the second century. Thus Ignatius speaks of Christ as "perfect man" as well as God, and therein anticipates the very formula of that later creed which bears (of course improperly) the name of Athanasius.

The fifth test of true development, "logical sequence," is the one which is, I fancy, most open to abuse in dealing with matters so much above us as theology. To infer correctly, the mind should be able to take in the full scope of a premiss. Even in mathematics it is always unsafe to treat inferences, which are correct when applied to ordinary cases, as justified when applied beyond the limits of quantitative measurement. It is true, as a rule, that if $a \times x = a \times y$, x must be $= y$, but the inference is quite false if a happens to be zero; otherwise every number would be equal to every other number, inasmuch as $2 \times 0 = 1000 \times 0$, but yet it does not in the least follow that $2 = 1000$. Just so inferences

from principles which appear true when we are dealing
with finite minds, are very apt to be quite false when
applied to an infinite mind. Indeed, all the juggling
with "the Absolute" and "the Infinite" which made
so much show of scientific reasoning in the late Dean
Mansel's *Bampton Lectures*, was really founded on the
fallacy that what would be a legitimate inference from
any statement as to a finite mind, would be an equally
legitimate inference from the same statement as to an
infinite mind.

Newman's chief illustration of the principle of "logical
sequence" as the test of a true development, is the
inference drawn from the condemnation of Arian forms
of doctrine, that there is so infinite a gulf between any
creature and God, that when once the true adoration of
any creature has been condemned, it becomes perfectly
safe to render homage to the saints and the Virgin
Mary, since it is no longer possible to suppose that they
are reverenced on their own account, but solely on
account of their close union with their Divine Master.
The charge of idolatry, he says, becomes unmeaning
after the condemnation of Arius. All good Catholics
know that the cults of the Virgin and the saints are
cults totally different in principle from religious worship.
They are far less to be called idolatrous than the homage
paid to a constitutional minister for his influence with
a monarch is to be called disloyal, whereas it is really
an implicit recognition of the true claim of loyalty.
The orthodoxy of the subordinate kind of homage is
a "logical" inference from the Church's anathema on
the proper adoration of a created being of any kind;
that is Newman's illustration of the test of "logical
sequence." But is it trustworthy? Is it true that the

anathema on Arianism rendered it safe to make so much of the intercession of the saints and the mother of Jesus Christ? Are not finite minds very apt to accept in the abstract a principle which they find it very difficult to realize in the concrete? Is it any less possible to preoccupy our minds with the influence and benevolence of beings like ourselves, to the virtual exclusion of the higher acts of worship, solely because we recognize in the abstract the infinitely superior power and love of God, than it is to fill up our minds with "the care of this world and the deceitfulness of riches," only because we recognize fully in the abstract that these have the power to choke the word and to suffocate its growth in the heart? Surely the real danger of the immense development which the Roman Catholic Church has given to the intercession of the Virgin Mary and the saints, is, that it tends to present to us the wills of beings who in knowledge and limitations are like ourselves, and who are supposed, at least by ignorant people, to be more influenced by our pertinacity of entreaty than God would be, as likely to urge upon God what He would otherwise refuse to do, and to try to impose upon Him by their entreaties their weaker forms of good-will; whereas, what ought to be impressed on the ignorant is, that the more completely any finite being has conformed himself to the will of God, the more resolutely would he refuse to intercede for any favour not intrinsically in harmony with the Divine providence. "Logical sequence" may be one test of true development, but unless you know that it has been faithfully applied to the higher and severer as well as the easier and milder aspects of the original teaching, it may be a test that leads you into all manner of worldly and degenerate developments.

The sixth test of true development, "preservative additions," corresponds in theology to the doctrine of the Law Courts, that they may assert their dignity and authority by punishing severely any "contempt of Court," or to the amendments adopted in some of the republican constitutions of the present day, which provide safeguards tending to prevent representative bodies from arrogating to themselves too much of the power of the whole people, of which a good example is the Swiss *referendum*, which overrules the action of the representative bodies by a census taken of the wishes of the whole people on some individual issue.

Newman gives as his first example of the "preservative additions" of religious development, one which seems to be hardly a very good example, because instead of its intention being to safeguard what has been already revealed, its intention is to reveal something fresh. "We know," he says, "that no temper of mind is acceptable in the Divine Presence but love; it is love which makes Christian fear differ from servile dread, and true faith differ from the faith of devils; yet in the beginning of the Christian life fear is the prominent evangelical grace, and love is but latent in fear, and has, in course of time, to be developed out of what seems its contradictory. Then when it is developed it takes that prominent place which fear held before, yet protecting, not superseding it. Love is added, not fear removed, and the mind is but perfected in grace by what seems a revolution. They that sow in tears reap in joy; yet afterwards still they are 'sorrowful,' though

'alway rejoicing.'"[1] That is exquisitely put, but surely
it degrades love to speak of its revelation as a mere
"preservative addition" to a Gospel of fear. I think,
perhaps, the best illustration which Newman gives of
the "preservative addition" is the foundation of the
Society of Jesus, for the protection and development of
the Catholic Church as it was in the century in which
Ignatius Loyola founded it, for it was clearly an addition,
and it did tend to preserve the Church as the Church
then was. Or perhaps his illustration of the use of the
cross as a symbol of holy war, to safeguard the Gospel of
peace, may be considered a still better instance in the
minds of those who regard the society founded by
Ignatius Loyola as preservative chiefly of existing
abuses. "If light has no communion with darkness,
or Christ with Belial, what has He to do with Moloch,
who would not call down fire on His enemies, and came
not to destroy but to save? Yet this seeming anomaly
is but one instance of a great law which is seen in
developments generally, that changes which appear at
first sight to contradict that out of which they grew,
are really its protection or illustration. Our Lord Himself is represented in the Prophets as a combatant
inflicting wounds while He received them, as coming
from Bozrah with dyed garments, sprinkled and red in
His apparel with the blood of His enemies; and whereas
no war is lawful but what is just, it surely beseems
that they who are engaged in so dreadful a commission
as that of taking away life at the price of their own,
should at least have the support of His Presence, and
fight under the mystical influence of His Name."[2]

[1] *Essay on Development*, chap. viii. section 2, p. 429, 1st edition.
[2] *Ibid.* chap. viii. section 2, p. 431.

I need give no illustration of Newman's seventh test of a true development, "chronic continuance." No one denies the historical continuity of the Roman Catholic Church. The question raised about her is not that, but whether she has fundamentally changed her type, her ideal. That she is, as the Protestants say, "incorrigible," is the best evidence that whether she has changed her type or not, she has continued to defy all the assaults made upon her.

This remarkable book in which the doctrine of development, treated many years afterwards so elaborately on its physiological side by Darwin, was anticipated in a theological treatise, concluded abruptly with a postscript evidently written after October 9th, 1845, when Newman was received at Littlemore by the Passionist Father Dominic into the Roman Catholic Church. The Oxford tradition says, that as Newman, month after month, stood at his desk writing the *Essay on Development,* he grew ever thinner and more transparent, till at last, when he suddenly dropped his pen and made up his mind that he had attained the fullest conviction that he must no longer delay his submission to Rome, on peril of sinning against light, you could almost have seen through him. The postscript to which I refer is one of those most characteristic passages by which Newman will be remembered as long as the English language endures. It is hardly as well known as the close of the last sermon which he preached as an Anglican, the sermon on "The Parting of Friends." Nor is it so exquisite in its pathos. But its absolute simplicity and appropriateness to the close of such an argument as this is most impressive. "Such," he wrote, "were the thoughts concerning 'The Blessed Vision of

Peace' of one whose long-continued petition had been that the Most Merciful would not despise the work of His own Hands, nor leave him to himself; while yet his eyes were dim, and his breast laden, and he could but employ Reason in the things of Faith. And now, dear reader, time is short, eternity is long. Put not from you what you have here found; regard it not as mere matter of present controversy; set not out resolved to refute it, and looking about for the best way of doing so; seduce not yourself with the imagination that it comes of disappointment, or disgust, or restlessness, or wounded feeling, or undue sensibility, or other weakness. Wrap not yourself round in the associations of years past, nor determine that to be truth which you wish to be so, nor make an idol of cherished anticipations. Time is short, eternity is long. Nunc dimittis servum tuum, Domine, secundum verbum tuum in pace, quia viderunt oculi mei salutare tuum." But the "nunc dimittis" was premature. Not the half of Newman's earthly career was run, though the portion of it most interesting to the non-Catholic world was at an end.

The late Canon Oakeley has given an account of the last day of Newman's Anglican life, which he calls the 9th October, 1845. Dr. Newman himself writes on the 8th October from Littlemore, that he is expecting the Passionist Father Dominic to arrive on that evening to receive him into the Catholic Church. Either Father Dominic was delayed a day, or Canon Oakeley was a day wrong[1] in his reckoning, for according to him it was the 9th October, a day of wild wind and pouring rain, on which Father Dominic, shabbily dressed in black,

[1] I see by a letter of Newman's to Mr. Allies, dated 9th October, 1845, that Canon Oakeley was a day wrong.

and dripping wet, arrived at Littlemore; and it was the 10th October, the day following his arrival, on which Newman was received into the Roman Catholic communion. On the evening of the Passionist father's arrival, Newman, as the story goes, flung himself at his feet, saying that he would not rise till the father had blessed him and received him into the Church of Christ. If so, his mind must have been wound up to a very high pitch of excitement before he could thus have thrown off the air of reserve and reticence so specially his own. The whole night was spent in prayer, and on the following day " the long gestation was accomplished," and Newman was born into the communion of the one Christian Church which has a historical continuity and an external organization as impressive and conspicuous as even his heart could desire for the depository of revealed truth.

Before I pass on to treat (very much more shortly) the story of Newman's life after the long period of doubt and hesitation was passed, and he had secured for himself the greater freedom of a position in the strength of which he had full confidence, I must make one remark on the general upshot of the essay which contained the fruits of his long hesitation and his elaborate research. What is the value of this *Essay on Development* for the world at large ? I think it has done a great deal towards showing that many of the later developments of the original teaching of Christ and His apostles are the genuine and natural outcome of the supernatural teaching given to the primitive Church, but that none the less the disposition to assert on the part of one branch of the Church too high a claim for its own infallibility and certainty of providential guidance, has always been visible. Newman's

own sermon, insisting on the great prophets granted to
a Church in open schism with the Jewish Church, the
Church of Samaria, is the most instructive illustration
of this disposition to over-estimate the infallibility of the
Church, which the Jewish revelation could supply.   It
is hardly possible to conceive that the Church of
Samaria could have been what the latest Jewish teaching held it to be, and could yet have been the Church
of such a prophet as Elijah.   And it is hardly possible
to conceive that the Church of England could be what
the Roman Catholic doctors describe it as being, and yet
the Church of such teachers as Bishop Butler or Newman himself.   Does not Newman throughout exaggerate
the claims of the Church to unity and infallibility ?   In
every age throughout the history of revelation there
are distinct traces of the precipitation of the orthodox
leaders of the Church in these matters.   In the *Essay
on Development*, Newman himself concedes to M. Guizot
that dogmatic principles were " not so well understood
and so carefully handled at first as they were afterwards.   In the early period we see traces of a conflict,
as well as of a variety, in theological elements, which
were in course of combination, but which required
adjustment and management before they could be used
with precision as one.   In a thousand instances of a
minor character, the statements of the early Fathers are
but tokens of the multiplicity of openings which the
mind of the Church was making into the treasure-house
of Truth ; real openings, but incomplete or irregular.
Nay, the doctrines even of heretical bodies are indices
and anticipations of the mind of the Church.   As the first
step in settling a point of doctrine is to raise and debate
it, so heresies in every age may be taken as the measure

of the existing state of thought in the Church, and of
the movement of her theology; they determine in what
way the current is setting, and the rate at which it
flows." [1]   Does not that apply as truly to the present
day as to any past day?   Can it be doubted for a
moment that the Roman Catholic Church's definitions
on the subject of the inspiration of Scripture have been
"incomplete and irregular," and, as I should say, directly
misleading?   Do not the most learned Catholics admit
and even maintain that "inspiration" must be taken
in quite a new sense before the inspiration of the
Scriptures "in all their parts" can be asserted with
even a semblance of truth?   Yet if that be so, that
means that the Roman Catholic Church has over-
leaped the truth in her deliberate definitions and formal
decrees, as well as in her *ad interim* pronouncements,
and that just as Elijah was taught that God had not
deserted the Church of Samaria in spite of schism and
idolatry, so God has not abandoned Churches which
Rome treats with mere contempt, in spite of their often
cold and degenerate worship.   Nevertheless, I sincerely
believe that Newman has shown that many of the
practices which were thought mere superstitions in the
Roman Catholic worship are natural developments of
the belief of the primitive Church, and not in the least
inconsistent with the pure rapture of the primitive
worship.   Is there truer Christian worship anywhere
than in the Church of Rome, in spite of the almost
greedy traditionalism with which her most famous
teachers seize upon doubtful and legendary elements of
pious rumour in bygone times to feed the appetite of
her contemplative orders?

[1] *Essay on Development*, p. 349, 1st edition, chap. **vi.** section 2.

CHAPTER X.

NEWMAN AS ROMAN CATHOLIC.

FROM the moment when Newman became a Roman
Catholic, the freest and happiest, though not perhaps
the most fascinating, epoch of his life may be said to
have commenced. I do not know that he ever again
displayed quite the same intensity of restrained and
subdued passion as found expression in many of his
Oxford sermons. But in irony, in humour, in eloquence,
in imaginative force, the writings of the later and, as
we may call it, the emancipated portion of his career
far surpass the writings of his theological apprentice-
ship. As my object has been to sketch the *growth* of
his convictions with much more care than their outcome, I will compress greatly my account of this second
half of Newman's life, which comprehends, however, the
most effective book he ever wrote, and certainly the
most remarkable of his controversial writings. For four
months after his conversion he continued to reside
generally at Littlemore, visiting Oscott at Cardinal
Wiseman's invitation in November 1845, only to be
confirmed, and not leaving Littlemore and the University of Oxford fully till February 1846. It was a
great wrench to him to separate himself from the
University to which he had always been warmly attached,

and where he had pleased himself by thinking that he
should live and die. And it was all the greater wrench
that his course was at this time so gravely misunder-
stood and so widely misrepresented amongst his old
friends and former colleagues. Indeed it was twenty
years after his conversion before he got the opportunity
of persuading the world that he had acted only on
conviction, and on conviction very slowly formed, very
anxiously reviewed, and indeed for a considerable time
deliberately suspended in order that he might adequately
test its force. For many years after his conversion
"the Protestant tradition," as he called it in his lectures
on "Catholicism in England," treated his conversion
as a sort of conspiracy deliberately devised for the sub-
version of the truth. In the first book which Newman
published after he became a Roman Catholic, *Loss and
Gain,* the story of a conversion to the Church of Rome,
he describes the effect produced by the rumours circulated against his young hero's Protestantism on the Vice-
principal and Principal of his College. He is refused
permission to reside in lodgings for the two terms before
he takes his degree on the ground of his suspected
Tractarianism; and on remarking to the Principal, Dr.
Bluett, that he cannot see what harm he could do by
residing in Oxford lodgings till Easter, Dr. Bluett cries
out in astonishment, "What, remain here, sir, with all
the young men about?" And on Charles Reding's
answering that he does not see why he should be unfit
company for them, "Dr. Bluett's jaw dropped, and his
eyes assumed a hollow aspect. 'You will corrupt their
minds, sir,' he said; 'you will corrupt their minds.'
Then he added in a sepulchral tone, which came from
the very depth of his inside, 'You will introduce them

to some subtle Jesuit, to some subtle Jesuit, Mr. Reding.'" This was very much the view taken for a long time of Dr. Newman's own proceedings by those who professed the "Protestantism of the Protestant Religion." It was part of a dark and deliberate plot against English Protestantism which had been long hatching, and would take long to expose. Newman went to Rome in October 1846, and returned to England on Christmas Eve, 1847. He soon determined to join the community of St. Philip Neri, the genial saint of the sixteenth century, who was called the Apostle of Rome during the earliest years of the Reformation. St. Philip was a saint of the world. It was a saying of his, "Oh, God, seeing that Thou art so infinitely lovable, why hast Thou given us but one heart to love Thee with, and this so little and so narrow?" What the ideal was which Newman set before himself on becoming an Oratorian of St. Philip's we can judge best from the character of St. Philip, which he afterwards quoted in the conclusion of his Dublin lectures on "the idea of a University," from Bacci, the biographer of St. Philip Neri. "He was all things to all men. He suited himself to noble and ignoble, young and old, subjects and prelates, learned and ignorant, and received those who were strangers to him with singular benignity, and embraced them with as much love and charity as if he had been a long while expecting them. When he was called upon to be merry he was so; if there was a demand upon his sympathy he was equally ready. He gave the same welcome to all: caressing the poor equally with the rich, and wearying himself to assist all to the utmost limits of his power. In consequence of his being so accessible and willing to receive

all comers, many went to him every day, and some continued for the space of thirty, nay forty years to visit
him very often both morning and evening, so that his
room went by the agreeable nickname of the home of
Christian mirth." In his own *Verses on Various
Occasions* [1] Newman has given a similar character of
" St. Philip in his school," drawn in words of his own—

> " This is the saint of gentleness and kindness,
>   Cheerful in penance, and in precept winning,
>   Patiently healing of their pride and blindness,
>   Souls that are sinning.
>
> This is the saint who, when the world allures us,
>   Cries her false wares, and opes her magic coffers,
>   Points to a better city, and secures us
>   With richer offers."

It was evidently the naturalness, the geniality, the
innocent mirth, and the social charm of St. Philip Neri
that made Newman so anxious to found an English
branch of the same order. His one idea, no doubt, both
in founding the order and in organizing it, was to get
a special hold on educated minds in religious perplexity,
but though when the Brompton Oratory was founded
as a branch from the Oratory at Birmingham, the
Brompton Oratorians made it more of their special work
to attack the slums of that part of London, Newman
in his work at Birmingham never in the least neglected
the poor. Indeed when in 1849 cholera broke out in a
severe form at Bilston, he and the late Father Ambrose
St. John undertook the work of visiting the sick and
dying in the most dangerous of the infected districts,
and discharged that difficult duty with the utmost zeal.
Still he never forgot that his special experience at
Oxford indicated that he was more likely to affect

[1] Page 306.

deeply the cultivated than the ignorant, and everything he published from the time of his conversion
to the present day has been almost exclusively addressed to minds of the same calibre and culture as
those with which he was familiar at Oxford.

Of his experience as a Catholic, *Loss and Gain*,
published in 1848, was the first fruit. It is hardly to
be called a story, and Newman stated when he gave it
to the public that it was " *not* founded upon fact." The
hero of it, who is converted from the English to the
Roman Catholic Church in the course of it, was not
meant for any living person, nor were any of the other
characters sketches from life. But the book has been
a great favourite with me, almost ever since its first
publication, partly for the admirable fidelity with which
it sketches young men's thoughts and difficulties, partly
for its happy irony, partly for its perfect representation
of the academical life and tone at Oxford. Charles
Reding, who is the hero of it, is delineated as a religious-
minded young man, who is eager for some credible and
definite assurance of what he ought to believe and what
he ought not. He is sure that there must be some final
authority as to what has been revealed, but he is utterly
perplexed by the conflict of views on the subject in his
own communion. " Wouldn't you be glad," says Reding
to a college friend, "if St. Paul could come to life? I've
often said to myself, ' Oh that I could ask St. Paul this
or that!'" "But the Catholic Church isn't St. Paul quite,
I guess," said Sheffield. " Certainly not ; but supposing
you did think it had the inspiration of an Apostle, as
the Roman Catholics do, what a comfort it would be to
know beyond all doubt what to believe about God, and
how to worship and please Him. I mean *you* said, ' I

can't believe this or that;' now you *ought* to have said,
'I can't believe the Pope has *power* to decide this or
that.' If he had, you ought to believe it, whatever it
is, and not to say, 'I can't believe.'" Here we see the
reflection of Newman's view of revelation as a coherent
system far above man's intellectual apprehensions, which
he is to believe as a matter of duty rather than for
its fascinating or subduing power over his mind. When
to this predisposition, which was certainly Newman's
own, we add Reding's craving for penance and ascetic
practices generally as at least a sort of satisfaction for
the deep sense of detestation with which he regarded
sin in himself, we need not feel at all surprised that
even though Reding is very far indeed from a duplicate
of Newman, he becomes gradually more and more repelled from the sober Anglican communion, and drawn
towards that which does lay down absolutely the dogmas
which it expects its children to accept, and does supply
them with penances and ascetic discipline in plenty. In
the course of the story there are many happy sketches
of Oxford society, such as, for example, the sketch of the
evangelical pietism which Mr. Freeborn pours forth at
Bateman's breakfast, or the sketch of the Rev. Dr. Brown-
side's prim and pompous Broad Church University
sermon, which said "one word in favour of Nestorius,
two for Abelard, three for Luther, that great spirit who
saw that churches, creeds, rites, forms, were nought in
religion, and that the inward spirit of *faith*, as he himself expressed it, was all in all." Again, there is one
very impressive passage *not* taken from Oxford life, in
which Newman makes the young Oxford convert who
precedes Reding in passing over to the Roman Catholic
Church insist on the vast difference between the

Protestant and the Roman Catholic conception of
worship, the former consisting in the pouring forth of
the human desire for Divine help, the latter in the
Mass, which is the "evocation" rather than the "invocation" of the Eternal, while the worshippers all
watch for a great event, indeed for a great advent,
waiting, like the paralytics beside the pool of Bethesda,
for "the moving of the water." Very striking and
beautiful too in its tenderness, and knowledge of human
nature, is Newman's delineation of the manner in which
Reding's mother takes leave of him when he announces
that he is going to join the Roman Catholic Church.
She holds out her hand coldly to him at first, reproaches
him with leaving his early friends, reproaches herself for
having made too much of him, and intimates that he is
leaving his own communion only because he likes leaving
it. When Charles replies, that in the Apostles' time
men were expected to give up all for Christ, she retorts
that this means that they of the English Church are
heathens, and she thanks him in a frigid manner for
such a comparison. Then she begins to refer to his
"dear father," her dead husband, and breaks down, and
he throws himself on his knees and lays his head in
her lap. The feelings of the mother altogether extinguish the hurt pride of the woman, and the scene
ends with her stroking his hair as she used to do when
a child, and letting her tears stream over his face.
Except in *Callista*, Newman has written nothing in the
form of fiction more touching than this passage. The
close of the book, where all the religious impostors
crowd into Charles's lodging, one after another, as
candidates for his adhesion, when it is rumoured that
he is dissatisfied with the Church of England, and is

leaving it for another communion, is a shade too farcical. It may perhaps represent some portion of Newman's personal experience, but then Newman was a distinguished man before he left the Anglican communion, and his movements would be watched by all sorts of religious speculators. Charles Reding could not possibly have been known to all these vigilant touters for religious adherents. He was a young Oxonian, and nothing more.

The next indication we have of the movements of Newman's mind after he joined the Roman Catholic communion, was the volume of *Sermons addressed to Mixed Congregations,* first published in 1849, and dedicated to the Right Rev. Nicholas Wiseman, not as yet at that time made a cardinal. These sermons have a definite tone and genius of their own; they have more in them of the enthusiasm of a convert than any other of Newman's publications, and altogether contain the most eloquent and elaborate specimens of his eloquence as a preacher, and of his sense, if I may so call it, of the religious advantages of his position as a spokesman of the great Church of Rome. They represent more adequately Dr. Newman as he was when he first felt himself "unmuzzled" (to use the phrase wired by Mr. Gladstone after the University of Oxford had rejected him, and he was no longer bound by the special etiquettes of a University representative), than any other of his writings; and though they have not to me quite the delicate charm of the reserve, and I might almost say the shy passion, of his Oxford sermons, they represent the full-blown blossom of his genius, while the former show it only in bud.

There, as in almost all his subsequent works, he gave

full rein to his wonderful power of irony, and even the
passages of tender eloquence, exquisite as they are, seem
to me inferior in force to the passages of scornful irony
in which he analyzes the worldly view of worldly things.
Take, for instance, the second sermon, that on "Neglect
of Divine Calls and Warnings," and compare the passage,
powerful and fearful as it is, in which he delineates
the agony of a soul which finds itself lost, with the
passage in which he delineates what the world is
meantime saying of the person "now no more," who
is undergoing the first pangs of this dreadful and endless suffering. "Impossible!" he supposes the lost one
to exclaim on hearing the Judge's sentence; "I a lost
soul! I separated from hope and from peace for ever!
It is not I of whom the Judge so spake! There is
a mistake somewhere; Christ, Saviour, hold Thy hand
—one minute to explain it! My name is Demas; I
am but Demas, not Judas, or Nicholas, or Alexander,
or Philetus, or Diotrephes. What! Eternal pain for
me! Impossible! it shall not be." And so he goes
on till the reader drops the book in horror and sickness
of heart.

Now take the suggestion of what the world may be
saying of him who is thus helplessly wrestling against
unendurable anguish, and refusing to believe in its
reality. "The man's name, perhaps, is solemnly chanted
forth, and his memory decently cherished among his
friends on earth. His readiness in speech, his fertility
in thought, his sagacity or his wisdom, are not forgotten. Men talk of him from time to time; they
appeal to his authority; they quote his words; perhaps
they even raise a monument to his name, or write his
history. 'So comprehensive a mind! such a power of

throwing light on a perplexed subject, and bringing ideas or facts into harmony!' 'Such a speech it was that he made on such and such an occasion; I happened to be present, and never shall forget it'; or, 'It was the saying of a very sensible man'; or, 'A great personage whom some of us knew'; or, 'It was a rule with a very worthy and excellent friend of mine, now no more'; or, 'Never was his equal in society, so just in his remarks, so versatile, so unobtrusive'; or, 'I was fortunate to see him once when I was a boy'; or, 'So great a benefactor to his country and to his kind'; or, 'His discoveries so great'; or, 'His philosophy so profound.' O vanity, vanity of vanities, all is vanity! What profiteth it, what profiteth it, his soul is in hell." Or take the passage in the sixth sermon, on "God's Will the end of Life," in which Dr. Newman paints the vulgar social ambitions of a citizen's life. "You think it the sign of a gentleman to set yourselves above religion; to criticize the religious and professors of religion; to look at Catholic and Methodist with impartial contempt; to gain a smattering of knowledge on a number of subjects; to dip into a number of frivolous publications, if they are popular; to have read the latest novel; to have heard the singer, and seen the actor of the day; to be up to the news; to know the names and, if so be, the persons of public men; to be able to bow to them; to walk up and down the street with your heads on high, and to stare at whatever meets you, and to say and do worse things, of which these are but the symbol. And this is what you conceive you have come upon earth for! The Creator made you, it seems, O my children, for this work and office, to be a bad imitation of polished ungodliness, to be a piece of tawdry and

faded finery, or a scent which has lost its freshness and
does but offend the sense." [1]

The extraordinary wealth of detail with which Newman conceives and realizes the various sins and miseries
of the human lot has, perhaps, never been illustrated in
all his writings with so much force as in the wonderful
sixteenth sermon on "The Mental Sufferings of our Lord
in His Passion"—a sermon before which even the rich-
ness and wealth of Jeremy Taylor's imagination looks
poor in the comparison. "It is the long history of a
world, and God alone can bear the load of it. Hopes
blighted, vows broken, lights quenched, warnings scorned,
opportunities lost; the innocent betrayed, the young
hardened, the penitent relapsing, the just overcome,
the aged failing; the sophistry of misbelief, the wilful-
ness of passion, the obduracy of pride, the tyranny of
habit, the canker of remorse, the wasting fever of
care, the anguish of shame, the pining of disappointment, the sickness of despair; such cruel, such pitiable
spectacles, such heartrending, revolting, detestable, mad-
dening scenes; nay, the haggard faces, the convulsed
lips, the flushed cheek, the dark brow of the willing
victims of rebellion, they are all before Him now, they
are upon Him and in Him. They are with Him
instead of that ineffable peace which has inhabited His
soul since the moment of His conception. They are
upon Him; they are all but His own; He cries to His
Father as if He were the criminal, not the victim; His
agony takes the form of guilt and compunction. He is
doing penance, He is making confession, He is exercising contrition with a reality and a virtue infinitely

_____
[1] *Discourses addressed to Mixed Congregations*, 3rd edition, pp.
132, 133.

greater than that of all saints and penitents together; for He is the One Victim for us all, the sole Satisfaction, the real Penitent, all but the real sinner." [1]

There you see the Catholic system taking full hold of Newman, and inspiring him with a sense of its authority and grandeur. Certainly no one could ever have gathered from the Gospels or Epistles that all this infinitude of anguish, quite alien to the special agony of the situation, and gathered out of all lands, from the east and from the west, from the north and from the south, and from all forms and phases of human transgression, piled itself up in the spirit of our Lord, and pressed upon Him, during His Passion, with the closeness of almost personal remorse. Yet so the Fathers of the Church had analyzed the mystery of the Passion, and so Newman unquestioningly accepted it. Whatever he has thought that he " ought " to believe, he has always found the means, not only to believe, but to interpret to himself with a unique vivacity and intensity of conception.

Never again did Newman give the rein so fully to what we may call the pious impressions, by the aid of which the Catholic Fathers have interpreted and illustrated the theology of the Church, as he did in this volume. In the sermons, for example, exquisite, even if too elaborate, as compositions, on *The Glories of Mary for the sake of her Son,* he almost rivalled the passion of Italian and French devotion to the mother of our Lord, and anticipated the dogma of the Immaculate Conception of the Virgin, some years before it had been defined. I know no passage in Newman which so

---

[1] *Discourses addressed to Mixed Congregations,* 3rd edition, pp. 394, 395.

thoroughly bewilders the Protestant imagination, in its unwillingness to accept vague tradition of the most distant and uncertain origin, as evidence for historic fact, as that in which he deals with the death of the mother of Christ. " Though she died as well as others, she died not as others die; for through the merits of her Son, by whom she was what she was, by the grace of Christ which in her had anticipated sin, which had filled her with light, which had purified her flesh from all defilement, she had been saved from disease and malady, and all that weakens and decays the bodily frame." Then he goes on to say:—"She died, but her death was a mere fact, not an effect; and when it was over, it ceased to be. She died that she might live; she died as a matter of form or (as I may call it) a ceremony, in order to fulfil what is called the debt of nature—not primarily for herself, or because of sin, but to submit herself to her condition, to glorify God, to do what her Son did; not, however, as her Son and Saviour, with any suffering for any special end; not with a martyr's death, for her martyrdom had been in living; not as an atonement, for man could not make it,—and One had made it, and made it for all,—but in order to finish her course and to receive her crown. And therefore she died in private. It became Him who died for the world to die in the world's sight; it became the great Sacrifice to be lifted up on high as a light that could not be hid. But she, the lily of Eden, who had always dwelt out of the sight of man, fittingly did she die in the garden's shade, and amid the sweet flowers in which she had lived. Her departure made no noise in the world. The Church went about her common duties—preaching, converting, suffering; there

were persecutions, there was fleeing from place to place,
there were martyrs, there were triumphs; at length
the rumour spread through Christendom that Mary was
no longer upon earth. Pilgrims went to and fro; they
sought for her relics, but they found them not. Did
she die at Ephesus? or did she die at Jerusalem?
Accounts varied, but her tomb could not be pointed
out, or if it was found, it was open; and instead of her
pure and fragrant body, there was a growth of lilies
from the earth which she had touched. So, inquirers
went home marvelling, and waiting for further light.
And then the tradition came wafted westward on the
aromatic breeze, how that when the time of her dis-
solution was at hand, and her soul was to pass in
triumph before the judgment-seat of her Son, the
Apostles were suddenly gathered together in one place,
even in the Holy City, to bear part in the joyful cere-
monial; how that they buried her with fitting rites;
how that the third day when they came to the tomb,
they found it empty, and angelic choirs with their glad
voices were heard singing day and night the glories of
their risen Queen. But however we feel towards the
detail of this history (nor is there anything in it which
will be unwelcome and difficult to piety), so much cannot
be doubted, from the consent of the whole Catholic
world and the revelations made to holy souls, that, as
is befitting, she is, soul and body, with her Son and God
in heaven, and that we are enabled to celebrate, not
only her death, but her Assumption." [1]

I gather from this, that Newman thinks the story
of the apostolic gathering to bury the Virgin Mary a

[1] *Discourses addressed to Mixed Congregations*, 3rd edition,
pp. 437—439.

pious opinion " not unwelcome or difficult to piety "
(though I should have supposed that a very great deal
which it is not *unwelcome* to pious people to believe
is yet very difficult for them to believe on what
amounts to hardly any evidence at all), but that he
regards the Assumption of her body to heaven as a
fact sufficiently attested by " the consent of the whole
Catholic world, and the revelations made to holy souls."
How does " the consent of the whole Catholic world "
to a tradition of which we cannot in the least trace the
origin, hidden as it is in the obscure depths of the first
century, justify us in accepting as historic fact that
of which there is absolutely not a morsel of historic
evidence ? Does the consent of the whole heroic
age of Greece guarantee the historic truth of the
labours of Hercules ? or the consent of the whole
mediæval age of Europe prove the historic truth of
the existence of fairies ? And have we any reason
to suppose that the assent of the Church of one century
to belief in a fact which could only have had any legitimate attestation in another century, is a good ground
for accepting that fact ? The " revelations given to
holy souls " might of course be evidence if there were
proof of the perfect truthfulness and sobriety of these
individual seers, and independent evidence of their
supernatural discernment of other facts, which at the
time at which they were discerned were beyond the
range of their senses, but afterwards verified. But what
is to ordinary minds marvellous in this passage is the
apparent acquiescence of so great a thinker as Newman
in the doctrine that " the mind of the Church " is not
only empowered to develop doctrine, but to attest minor
historic facts of which it has had no evidence apparently,

and this on no better ground than that such facts would
not be unwelcome to it if the evidence were forthcoming.
Surely the readiness, and even eagerness, with which
it assimilates a tradition of which no one can find the
smallest trace in the only age in which, if a genuine
tradition at all, it must have originated, is a ground for
distrust rather than for trust.   How can Newman say
that a good Catholic "ought" to believe a fact of this
kind,—not even a "dogmatic fact," not even a fact intimately bound up with a cardinal doctrine of the
Church,—on the strength merely of the consent of the
Church in a devotional but uncritical age, to celebrate
a festival of the Assumption?   One might as well say
that an Oxonian of University College "ought" to
believe that King Alfred founded that college, because
such a belief is grateful to the minds of University
College men, though the best historians regard it as
quite baseless.   To me this is just the most suspicious
of all the aspects of Roman Catholicism, that the Church
shows such avidity in accepting as facts, devotional
dreams of apparently very late and ambiguous origin.
Some French Roman Catholics use a devotion to St.
Mary Magdalene which contains entreaties for her
intercession addressed in the following terms,—"Vous
qui avez passé de long jours dans une solitude affreuse
vivant miraculeusement—vous qui sept fois par jour,
étiez portée par les anges au sommet du ciel," &c.
Now I do not suppose for a moment that these devotions
have the authority of the Church, in the sense in which
the teaching that the body of the mother of our Lord
was raised on the third day and ascended to heaven
has that authority.   But I do say that utterly
unauthentic statements of this kind are welcomed

generally in Catholic devotion, and that, though they
may contain harmless as well as baseless assertions
considered in themselves, it is not a perfectly harmless
state of mind to be eager to feed the imagination on
dreams of which there is no evidence at all, beyond the
readiness of popular assemblies to adopt as serious truth
the statements made in picturesque legends of which
the origin is entirely lost. I can understand, and to a
certain extent I believe, that inspiration not only guides
and overrules our ideal of the spiritual life, but moulds
the attitude of the Church to whom it is revealed, and
guards the development of its mind in bringing out
the meaning of doctrine to questioning believers.
But the contention that the Church may bear authoritative witness for the first time in a late age to facts
of which no early trace remains, to facts not only not
admitting of the smallest comparison in the amount of
evidence producible for them with the facts of the
Gospel, but, on the contrary, having upon them the
most marked characteristics of popular legends, seems
to me one of the most startling to which Newman ever
gave cordial assent. We might almost as well regard
the old village plays on St. George and the Dragon
as satisfactory evidence of that mythical contest. Is
it not true that the Roman Catholic disposition to treat
opinions as "pious" for which there is nothing approaching to evidence, lends sanction to the doctrine that
"the wish to believe" in the reality of a certain event
is a good reason for actually believing in it? This is
the side of Newman's mind with which the greater
number of his fellow - countrymen feel the greatest
possible difficulty in sympathizing.

The next landmark in Newman's history as a Roman

Catholic was his delivery and publication in 1850 of the *Lectures on Anglican Difficulties*, delivered in the Oratory in King William Street, Strand, where Toole's Theatre now stands, at all or almost all of which I was present as a young man. In matter and style alike these lectures were marked by all the signs of his singular literary genius. They were simpler and less ornate than the *Sermons addressed to Mixed Congregations*, and more exquisite in form as well as more complete in substance than the *Essay on Development*, which was written under the heavy pressure of the dreaded and anticipated rupture between himself and the Church of his baptism. I think the *Lectures on Anglican Difficulties* was the first book of Newman's generally read amongst Protestants, in which the measure of his literary power could be adequately taken. In the Oxford sermons there had been of course more room for the expression of religious feeling of a higher type, and frequently there had been more evidence of depth and grasp of mind; but here was a great subject with which Newman was perfectly intimate, giving the fullest scope to his powers of orderly and beautiful exposition, and opening a far greater range to his singular genius for gentle and delicate irony than anything which he had previously written. It is a book, however, which adds but little to our insight into his mind, though it adds much to our estimate of his powers, and I must pass it by with only brief notice. I shall never forget the impression which his voice and manner, which opened upon me for the first time in these lectures, made on me. Never did a voice seem better adapted to persuade without irritating. Singularly sweet, perfectly free from any dictatorial note, and yet rich in all the cadences proper to the expression of pathos, of wonder, and of ridicule, there was still nothing in it that any one could properly describe as insinuating, for its simplicity, and frankness, and freedom from the half-smothered notes which express indirect purpose, was as remarkable as its sweetness, its freshness, and its gentle distinctness. As he described the growth of his disillusionment with the Church of England, and compared it to the transformation which takes place in fairy tales when the magic castle vanishes, the spell is broken, "and nothing is seen but the wild heath, the barren rock, and the forlorn sheep-walk," no one could have doubted that he was describing with perfect truth the change that had taken place in his own mind. "So it is with us," he said, "as regards the Church of England, when we look in amazement on that we thought so unearthly, and find so commonplace or worthless. Then we perceive that aforetime we have not been guided by reason, but biased by education, and swayed by affection. We see in the English Church, I will not merely say, no descent from the first ages, and no relationship to the Church in other lands, but we see no body politic of any kind; we see nothing more or less than an establishment, a department of government, or a function or operation of the State—without a substance,—a mere collection of officials, depending on and living in the supreme civil power. Its unity and personality are gone, and with them its power of exciting feelings of any kind. It is easier to love or hate an abstraction than so tangible a frame-work or machinery."[1]

[1] *Lectures on Anglican Difficulties*, p. 7, 2nd edition.

This is, of course, an exaggerated view. It is not true that the State can do what it pleases with the English Church, can modify its theology or change its liturgy at will; but it is still less true that the Church can do as she will without the consent of the State. The English Church is an amalgam of two alien organizations, not the organized form of a religious society. "Elizabeth," said Newman, "boasted that she 'tuned its pulpits'; Charles forbade discussions on predestination; George on the Holy Trinity; Victoria allows differences on Holy Baptism." The dialogue which Newman constructed in his fourth lecture between the Tractarian and the State, to illustrate this view, was one of the most effective pieces of irony I ever heard. I may briefly condense it. "Why should any man in Britain," asks a Tract, "fear or hesitate boldly to assert the authority of the Bishops and pastors of the Church on grounds strictly evangelical and spiritual?" "Reverend Sir," answered the Primate to a protest against a Bishop elect accused of heresy, "it is not within the bounds of any authority possessed by me to give you an opportunity of proving your objections; finding therefore nothing in which I could act in compliance with your remonstrance, I proceeded, in the execution of my office, to obey her Majesty's mandate for Dr. Hampden's consecration in the usual form." "Are we contented," asks another Tract, "to be accounted the mere creation of the State, as schoolmasters and teachers may be, as soldiers or magistrates, or other public officers? Did the State make us? Can it unmake us? Can it send out missionaries? Can it arrange dioceses?" "William the Fourth," answers the first magistrate of the State, "by the grace of God of the United Kingdom of Great Britain and Ireland, King, Defender of the Faith, to all to whom these presents shall come, greeting; we having great confidence in the learning, morals, and probity of our well-beloved and venerable William Grant Broughton, do name and appoint him to be Bishop and ordinary pastor of the See of Australia." " Confirmation is an ordinance," says the Tract, " in which the Bishop wit- nesses Christ. . . . The Bishop is His figure and likeness when he lays his hands on the heads of children. Then Christ comes to them to confirm in them the grace of baptism." " And we do hereby give and grant to the said Bishop of Australia," proceeds his Majesty, " and his successors, Bishops of Australia, full power and authority to confirm those that are baptized and come to years of discretion." " Moreover," says the Tract, " the Bishop rules the Church here below, as Christ rules it above. . . . He is Christ's instrument." " And we do by these presents give and grant to the said Bishop and his successors, Bishops of Australia, full power and authority to admit into the holy orders of deacon and priest respectively any person whom he shall deem duly qualified." " The Bishop speaks in me," says the Tract, "as Christ wrought in him, and as God sent Christ. Thus the whole plan of salvation hangs together —Christ the true mediator; His servant the Bishop, His earthly likeness; mankind the subjects of His teaching; God the author of salvation. And the Queen answers, 'We do hereby signify to the most reverend Father in God, William, Lord Archbishop of Canterbury, our nomination of the said Augustus, requiring, and by the faith and love whereby he is bound unto us, command- ing the said most reverend Father in God to ordain

and consecrate the said Augustus.' And the consecrated prelate echoes from across the ocean against
the Catholic pastor of the country, 'Augustus, by the
grace of God and the favour of Queen Victoria, Bishop.'"[1]

Indeed this whole lecture delivers one of the most
powerful attacks ever opened on the Anglican theory
of the Church as independent of the State. Not less
powerful was Newman's delineation, in the fifth lecture,
of the collapse of the Anglican theory of the Church
when applied to practice. The Anglicans, he said,
"had reared a goodly house, but their foundations were
falling in. The soil and the masonry both were bad.
The Fathers would protect 'Romanists' as well as
extinguish Dissenters. The Anglican divines would
misquote the Fathers and shrink from the very doctors
to whom they appealed. The Bishops of the seventeenth century were shy of the Bishops of the fourth,
and the Bishops of the nineteenth were shy of the
Bishops of the seventeenth. The Ecclesiastical Courts
upheld the sixteenth century against the seventeenth,
and, unconscious of the flagrant irregularities of Protestant clergymen, chastised the mild misdemeanours
of Anglo-Catholic. Soon the living rulers of the
Establishment began to move. There are those who,
reversing the Roman maxim, are wont to shrink from
the contumacious, and to be valiant towards the sub-
missive; and the authorities in question gladly availed
themselves of the power conferred on them by the
movement against the movement itself. They fear-
lessly handselled their Apostolical weapons against the
Apostolical party. One after another, in long succession,

---

[1] *Lectures on Anglican Difficulties*, pp. 89—91, 2nd edition.

they took up their song and their parable against it.
It was a solemn war-dance which they executed round
victims, who, by their very principles, were bound hand
and foot, and could only eye, with disgust and perplexity, this most unaccountable movement on the
part of these 'holy Fathers, the representatives of the
Apostles and the Angels of the Churches.' It was the
beginning of the end." [1]

The lectures were much more powerful in attack than
in defence. Those of which it was the object to show
that the Anglican Church was essentially Erastian, and
was not one which could ever satisfy the ideal of the
Tractarians, were simply demonstrative; the lectures of
which it was the intention to remove the objections felt
towards the Roman Catholic communion were partly
defective, partly inadequate. They did not deal at all
with what seems to me the greatest of all objections
to the Roman Catholic Church, the indifference she
shows to reasonable criticisms, even in her most solemn
acts, such as the sanction given to utterly unhistorical
facts in the feast of the Assumption of the Virgin Mary,
and the sanction given to the doctrine of the plenary
inspiration of the Scriptures in the decrees of the
Council of Trent and (subsequently) of the Council of
the Vatican. On the other hand, the eighth and ninth
lectures on the " Political state of Catholic countries no
prejudice to the sanctity of the Church," and the
" Religious character of Catholic countries no prejudice
to the sanctity of the Church," raise, I think, at least as
many difficulties as they remove. And in effect they
almost concede that comparative want of self-reliance

---

[1] *Lectures on Anglican Difficulties*, pp. 125-26, lecture v.

and self-control in matters both political and religious which certainly characterizes Catholic countries, as distinguished from those Catholic communities which exist in the heart of Protestant countries, and which are surrounded on all sides by religious opponents. Newman's apology for the political and religious state of Ireland as given in 1850 seems even less effective, indeed *much* less effective, when read in 1890 than it seemed then.   Almost all that Ireland has gained since 1850, she has gained by the resolute ignoring of Catholic principles ; and all that she has lost, she has lost by the resolute ignoring of Catholic principles. And though the gain may be considerable politically, I fear the moral loss far outweighs the political gain.

The *Lectures on Catholicism in England*, delivered and published in the year of the first great Exhibition, 1851, need not detain me for more than a few lines. They represent very effectively the force of the " Protestant tradition " as it was in 1851, though what was truly enough said then, now enormously exaggerates the force of that tradition, the difference being largely due to Newman's personal influence, exerted partly through the publication of these lectures, though in a far greater degree through the publication of his religious autobiography thirteen years later.   The *Lectures on Catholicism in England* depicted very powerfully the nonsensical and fanatical side of Protestantism, though they did not do justice to the grounds of offence found by sober and accurate-minded men in the teaching of the Roman Catholic Communion.   There are passages in these lectures which pass the limits of irony, and approach the region of something like controversial farce, yet farce of no common order of power.   Where, for

example, could we find a more exquisitely humorous
and yet a truer description than Newman gives of
the mode in which the re-establishment of the Roman
Catholic hierarchy in this country had been received by
English Protestants in the preceding year? "Heresy,
and scepticism, and infidelity, and fanaticism may
challenge" the Established Church, he said, "in vain;
but fling upon the gale the faintest whisper of Catholicism, and it recognizes by instinct the presence of its
connatural foe.   Forthwith, as during the last year,
the atmosphere is tremulous with agitation, and dis-
charges its vibrations far and wide.   A movement
is in birth which has no natural crisis or resolution.
Spontaneously the bells of the steeples begin to sound.
Not by an act of volition, but by a sort of mechanical
impulse, bishop and dean, archdeacon and canon, rector
and curate, one after another, each on his high tower,
off they set, swinging and booming, tolling and chiming,
with nervous intenseness, and thickening emotion, and
deafening volume, the old ding-dong which has scared
town and country this weary time; tolling and chiming
away, jingling and clamouring, and ringing the changes
on their poor half-dozen notes, all about 'the Popish
aggression,' 'insolent and insidious,' 'insidious and insolent,' 'insolent and atrocious,' 'atrocious and insolent,'
'atrocious, insolent, and ungrateful,' 'ungrateful, insolent, and atrocious,' 'foul and offensive,' 'pestilent and
horrid,' 'subtle and unholy,' 'audacious and revolting,'
'contemptible and shameless,' 'malignant,' 'frightful,'
'mad,' 'meretricious,' bobs (I think the ringers call
them), bobs, and bobs royal, and triple bob-majors and
grandsires—to the extent of their compass, and the full
ring of their metal, in honour of Queen Bess, and to

the confusion of the Pope and the princes of the Church." [1]

Probably the most important of the immediate results of this course of lectures was the action for libel brought by Dr. Achilli against Newman, for the picture painted of him in the fifth lecture on "The Popular Inconsistency of the Protestant View." Dr. Achilli, who professed to be a convert from Romanism, was accused by the Papal Government of a grossly irregular life, and Newman used the offences of which that Government believed him to be guilty as illustrations of the sources from which the Protestant tradition derives its knowledge of the Catholic faith. The charges were flatly denied by Dr. Achilli, who declared that his real sin in the eyes of the Papal Government was his heterodoxy, and though Newman brought a large number of witnesses to support his statements, the British jury, directed by the late Lord Campbell, was not disposed to be satisfied with evidence which ran counter to the Protestant tradition of the day. The general impression even of non-Catholic culture at the time was not favourable to the impartiality of Lord Campbell's charge, but it fell in with the temper of the middle classes of that day, and gave the jury a good excuse for their verdict, that the main accusations had not been justified to their satisfaction. The costs amounted to £12,000, and were paid by a Catholic subscription from all parts of the world; even the soberer view among Protestants was not for the most part in harmony with the verdict or with the attitude of the judge. Nevertheless, another period of eleven years elapsed before an attack

[1] *Lectures on Catholicism in England*, 1st edition, lecture ii., pp. 73, 74.

of a different character, proceeding from the pen of a very different assailant, gave Dr. Newman the opportunity of achieving the greatest triumph of his life, so far as regards his influence over men of theological tendencies quite different from his own.

In 1852 Newman was sent to Dublin, to inaugurate there the Roman Catholic University teaching, which has been struggling into existence—more or less feebly —ever since. The lectures, or "Discourses" rather, on *The Idea of a University*, which he delivered and published on this occasion, are full of graceful and instructive thought; and indeed gave an impulse to the comprehension of true University culture, which had, I believe, a very great effect in stimulating the reforms which soon afterwards took place in the Universities of Oxford and Cambridge, though they have not often been traced home to this origin. The reason why the influence of these remarkable "Discourses" (they were too much of academical "Discourses," to my mind, and therefore did not do full justice to that exquisite ease of manner which is usually the greatest literary charm of Dr. Newman's writings) on the movements which so soon afterwards took place at Oxford and Cambridge was missed, was that their chief design—namely, to bring out the importance of Theology as the uniting bond of all the sciences—was directly in antagonism to the reforming movement in the English Universities, where theological considerations — and those of a dry and formal kind—had long been more mixed up with the motives determining the choice of teachers in other branches of study, than they ought to have been. But what is forgotten is, that these discourses enforced with the utmost power the true purpose of liberal education, that it is a pursuit of knowledge for the sake of knowledge, and not for the value of any of the fruits or applications of knowledge, however important. Newman earnestly repudiated the notion that the acquisition of knowledge is merely subsidiary even to religion. On the contrary, his general position throughout these discourses is, that Theology is essential to true University study, because it is a branch of true knowledge, and indeed the most real and the most important of all the branches of true knowledge, since it harmonizes and connects all the other studies and sciences, and gives them their due subordination in relation to the purposes of life.

At that time Newman had a difficult task to achieve in persuading the Roman Catholic prelates of Ireland that University teaching, in the sense in which Newman understood and advocated it, was of the greatest possible importance to all true Catholics who had to deal with the greater intellectual forces of the world, besides that, in fact, such culture gives them for the first time true possession of their own minds. The Catholic prelates knew how much there is in liberal education, of a tendency to subvert faith, and this they justly feared. They did not know how much there is in the world, *without* liberal education, that has the same tendency in a still higher degree; they had not grasped the fact that the uneducated mind is utterly unable to understand the true proportions of things, and magnifies immensely the significance of the first difficulties or paradoxes with which, in the study of religion, it is brought face to face. To prelates in such a state of mind as this there must have been food for very useful and perhaps rather painful reflection in such considerations as these which

the Rector of their infant University pressed upon them
with his wonted vivacity and energy. "Even if we
could, still we should be shrinking from our plain duty,
gentlemen, did we leave out literature from education.
For why do we educate except to prepare for the
world? Why do we cultivate the intellect of the
many beyond the first elements of knowledge, except
for this world? Will it be much matter in the world
to come whether our bodily health, or whether our intellectual strength, was more or less, except of course as
this world is in all its circumstances a trial for the next?
If then a University is a direct preparation for this
world, let it be what it professes. It is not a convent;
it is not a seminary; it is a place to fit men of the
world for the world. We cannot possibly keep them
from plunging into the world, with all its ways and
principles and maxims, when their time comes; but
we can prepare them against what is inevitable; and it
is not the way to learn to swim in troubled waters never
to have gone into them. Proscribe, I do not merely say
particular authors, particular works, particular passages,
but Secular Literature as such; cut out from your
class-books all broad manifestations of the natural man;
and these manifestations are waiting for your pupil's
benefit at the very doors of your lecture-room in living
and breathing substance. They will meet him there in
all the charm of novelty, and all the fascination of
genius or of amiableness. To-day a pupil, to-morrow
a member of the great world; to-day confined to the
lives of the Saints, to-morrow thrown upon Babel—
thrown on Babel without the honest indulgence of wit
and humour and imagination having ever been permitted to him, without any fastidiousness of taste

wrought into him, without any rule given him for
discriminating 'the precious from the vile,' beauty
from sin, the truth from the sophistry of nature, what
is innocent from what is poison.   You have refused him
the masters of human thought, who would in some
sense have educated him, because of their incidental
corruption; you have shut up from him those whose
thoughts strike home to our hearts, whose words are
proverbs, whose names are indigenous to all the world,
who are the standard of the mother tongue, and the
pride and boast of their countrymen, Homer, Ariosto,
Cervantes, Shakespeare, because the old Adam smelt
rank in them; and for what have you reserved him ?
You have given him a ' liberty unto' the multitudinous
blasphemy of his day; you have made him free of its
newspapers, its reviews, its magazines, its novels, its
controversial pamphlets, of its Parliamentary debates,
its law proceedings, its platform speeches, its songs,
its drama, its theatre, of its enveloping, stifling atmosphere of death.   You have succeeded but in this—in
making the world his University."[1]

I have often wished that we could have had as
frank an account of the impression made upon Newman
by his continuous residence in Dublin for several years,
and his intercourse with the Irish prelates, as we have
of that little tour of Carlyle in Ireland, which took place
about the time of Newman's first residence there.   Of
course we never shall have any such record, for Newman
was too prudent as well, I imagine, as too modest to
write down cursory impressions of the value of which
he himself would have been no doubt extremely sceptical.

[1] Discourse IX, § 8.

But if we could have such a record, it might, I think, considerably outweigh the value of Carlyle's brilliant but inconsiderate and rather violent characterizations of the Irish people and Irish scenes.

It was while he was still in Ireland that Newman finished the little work which seems to me the most perfect and singular in spiritual beauty, excepting perhaps the *Dream of Gerontius,* that he has written, *Callista.* "It is an attempt," he said in his preface, "to imagine and express the feelings and mutual relations of Christians and heathens at the period to which it belongs,[1] and it has been undertaken as the nearest approach which the author could make to a more important work suggested to him from a high ecclesiastical quarter." *Callista* was begun, he tells us, in the early spring of 1848, probably soon after *Loss and Gain* was finished; but after sketching the character and fortunes of Juba, the half-African youth (whose father, a Roman soldier, is a languid Christian, while his mother is a heathen sorceress), in whom Newman made a powerful attempt to realize the significance of demoniacal possession as it was conceived and held in the early centuries of the Christian era, he stopped, as he says, "from sheer inability to devise personages or incidents." "He suddenly resumed the thread of his story shortly after St. Mary Magdalene's day," in 1855, and when it was finished it was published anonymously. The secret of the authorship, however, oozed out, and an edition was soon published with Newman's name. It has never attained the popularity which it seems to me to deserve, partly perhaps because the framework of the story involves a certain amount of

[1] The middle of the third century.

NEWMAN AS ROMAN CATHOLIC.

antiquarian disquisition, which fatigues ordinary readers
—like the idol-seller's discourse to his nephew on the
different kinds of Roman marriage—and partly because
the sentiment of the book is of too exalted a kind to
make its way to the heart of a hasty reader in search of
exciting incident. Yet it is not wanting in very striking
and even sensational incidents. The invasion of the
locusts is described with all the imaginative power of a
great genius; the sudden madness which seizes upon
Juba when his mother curses and bewitches him, is
painted with extraordinary force; and it would be
hard to delineate a popular riot involving persecution
and martyrdom with more strength and pathos.

After all, however, the great triumph of the book is
the delineation of the fair Greek, herself a sculptor of
idols, who has so passionate a love of Greek idealism,
and so deep a sense that there is some vision of truth
beyond the Greek idealism for which her heart yearns
in vain. The strange and apparently almost capricious
resentment with which she meets Agellius's offer of
marriage, because it lowers him in her eyes by making
it evident that his Christian faith was but an unreal
affair, and quite consistent with the ordinary devotion
to the passions and affections of time and sense of
which she had seen so much, is painted with the full
force of Newman's genius. I know nothing in all
fiction more delicate, more spiritual, more fascinating
than the story of Callista's conversion and death. The
reproaches she heaps on Agellius for not clearly discriminating between his love for her and his wish for
her conversion,—which she calls "speaking one word
for his Master and two for himself,"—and the deep
disappointment with which she discovers, or fancies she

discovers, that Agellius is after all a good deal more
taken up with her and her beauty than with the faith
which she had hoped to have found the one great reality
of his existence, seem to me in many respects better ex-
pressions of the true passion and significance of Newman's own unique and single-hearted life, than anything
else which he has written. "'If, as you imply,' she
says, 'my wants and aspirations are the same as yours,
what have you done towards satisfying them? What
have you done for that Master towards whom you now
propose to lead me? No,' she continued, starting up,
'you have watched those wants and aspirations for
yourself, not for Him; you have taken interest in
them, you have cherished them, as if you were the
author, you the object of them. You profess to believe
in One true God, and to reject every other; and now
you are implying that the Hand, the Shadow of that
God is on my mind and heart. Who is this God?
where? how? in what? Oh, Agellius, you have stood
in the way of Him, ready to speak of yourself, using
Him as a means to an end.' 'O, Callista,' said Agellius
in an agitated voice, when he could speak, 'do my ears
hear aright? do you really wish to be taught who
the true God is?' 'No; mistake me not,' she cried
passionately, 'I have no such wish. I could not be
of your religion. Ye gods, how have I been deceived!
I thought every Christian was like Chione. I thought
there could not be a cold Christian. Chione spoke as
if a Christian's first thoughts were good-will to others,
as if his state were of such blessedness that his dearest
heart's wish was to bring others into it. Here is a
man who, so far from feeling himself blest, thinks I
can bless him; comes to me, me, Callista, a herb of the

field, a poor weed exposed to every wind of heaven
and shrivelling before the fierce sun—to me he comes
to repose his heart upon. But as for any blessedness
he has to show me, why, since he does not feel any
himself, no wonder he has none to give away. I
thought a Christian was superior to time and place,
but all is hollow. Alas! alas! I am young in life to feel
the force of that saying with which sages go out of it,
"Vanity and hollowness!" Agellius, when I first heard
you were a Christian, how my heart beat! I thought
of her who was gone; and at first I thought I saw her
in you, as if there had been some magical sympathy
between you and her; and I hoped that from you I
might have learned more of that strange strength which
my nature needs, and which she told me she possessed.
Your words, your manner, your looks were altogether
different from others who came near me. But so it
was; you came and you went, and came again; I
thought it reserve, I thought it timidity, I thought it
the caution of a persecuted sect; but oh! my disappointment when first I saw in you indications that
you were thinking of me only as others think, and felt
towards me as others may feel; that you were aiming
at me, not at your God; that you had much to tell of
yourself, but nothing of Him! Time was I might have
been led to worship you, Agellius; you have hindered
it by worshipping *me.*'" [1]

And when she is in prison on suspicion of being a
Christian, and has refused, she hardly knows why, to
burn incense to the Emperor, and a Greek philosopher
has been persuaded to come to her cell to convince

[1] Chapter xi.

her of the unreasonableness of her proceeding, the same fine passion bursts forth again with still more definiteness and significance. "After a time Callista said, 'Polemo, do you believe in one God?' 'Certainly,' he answered, 'I believe in one eternal, self-existing something.' 'Well,' she said, 'I feel that God within my heart, I feel myself in His presence. He says to me, "Do this, don't do that." You may tell me that this dictate is a mere law of my nature, as to joy or to grieve. I cannot understand this. No, it is the echo of a person speaking to me. Nothing shall persuade me that it does not ultimately proceed from a person external to me. It carries with it its proof of its Divine origin. My nature feels towards it as towards a person. When I obey it, I feel a satisfaction; when I disobey, a soreness, just as I feel in pleasing or offending some revered friend. So you see, Polemo, I believe in what is more than a mere " something." I believe in what is more real to me than sun, moon, stars, and the fair earth, and the voice of friends. You will say, Who is He? Has He ever told you anything about Himself? Alas! no! the more's the pity! But I will not give up what I have because I have not more. An echo implies a voice, a voice a speaker. That speaker I love and I fear.' Here she was exhausted, and overcome too, poor Callista, with her own emotions. 'O that I could find Him,' she exclaimed passionately. 'On the right hand and on the left I grope, but touch Him not. Why dost Thou fight against me, why dost Thou scare and perplex me, O, First and only Fair? I have Thee not and I need Thee.' She added, 'I am no Christian, you see, or I should have found Him; or at least I should say I had found Him.' 'It is hopeless,' said Polemo to Aristo, in much disgust, and with some hauteur of manner; 'she is too far gone. You should not have brought her to this place.'"[1]   That is, I think, something more than a delineation of "the mutual relation of Christians and heathens" in the third century. It is a delineation of that pure flame of passion in Newman's own heart and life which made him "rest in the thought of two, and two only, supreme and luminously self-evident beings—myself and my Creator."

To me *Callista* has always seemed the most completely characteristic of Newman's books. Many of them express with greater power his intellectual delicacy of insight, and his moral intensity, but none, unless it be *The Dream of Gerontius*, expresses as this does the depth of his spiritual passion, the singular wholeness, unity, and steady concentration of purpose connecting all his thoughts, words, and deeds. And yet it is not, and I think will never be, the most popular of his books. That fate was reserved for his reply to Mr. Kingsley's attack on him on account of the sanction he had lent, or which Mr. Kingsley supposed him to have lent, to the doctrine that "truth is no virtue." I have often wondered that Kingsley had never been sensible of the fascination of Newman's deep religious nature, an intensity of which there was certainly no slight measure in himself. He too, like Newman, was a genuine poet, though a poet of a very different type. Again, he too, like Newman, had felt the deepest interest in "the mutual relations of Christians and heathens" in the early centuries of Christianity, and had attempted, as Newman did, to delineate it in his story of *Hypatia*.

[1] *Callista*, chap. xxvii.

Q

But there was something headlong about Kingsley, as there is something essentially reserved and reticent about Newman, and there, I fancy, was the secret of the repulsion between them. Kingsley's ideal always tended somewhat towards surrender to the glory of action and passion, towards embodiment in life, towards glow, and emphasis, and self-expansion. He had an odd theory, too, that a hearty English squire who does his duty, not only to the land, but to the tenants and the labourers on his estate, is the nearest thing to a saint which the world can produce, and it is not easy to imagine any ideal more different from Newman's. As far as I can judge, Kingsley and Newman have both been supremely truthful men, and Newman, I should say, though far the subtler and less easily understood of the two, not by any means less truthful than his rather random assailant.

In *Macmillan's Magazine* for January 1864, which (as usual with January magazines) was published before Christmas 1863, Mr. Kingsley, in a review of Froude's *History of England*, had written, "Truth for its own sake had never been a virtue with the Roman clergy. Father Newman informs us that it need not be, and on the whole ought not to be; that cunning is the weapon which Heaven has given to the saints wherewith to withstand the brute male force of the wicked world which marries and is given in marriage. Whether his notion be doctrinally correct or not, it is at least historically so." The reference, as Mr. Kingsley afterwards stated, was to Newman's sermon on "Wisdom and Innocence," sermon 20 in the Oxford volume on *Subjects of the Day*, which was preached on February 19th, 1843, of which the text would certainly have been, as I remarked at the time of the discussion about Kingsley's dictum, far more paradoxically open to that imputation than any interpretation of it given by Dr. Newman—"Behold, I send you forth as sheep in the midst of wolves; be ye therefore wise as serpents, and harmless as doves."

Newman of course noticed that amongst the lower races of animals to which our Lord alluded in this precept, "the weak" are compensated for their weakness by fleetness, or by the difficulty of discriminating them from the localities to which they resort, or by "some natural cunning." "Brute force is countervailed by flight, brute passion by prudence and artifice." But this was said exclusively of the instincts of the weaker animals. Of men he expressly said that all sinful means of defence are forbidden to the weak, and many are forbidden which would not have been sinful had they not been forbidden. He admitted that Christians had been tempted "to the abuse instead of the use of Christian wisdom, to be wise without being harmless," and this he condemned. On the other hand, Christians in times of persecution are perfectly right in observing prudence and reticence. "Other men make a great clamour and lamentation over their idols; there is no mistaking that they have lost them, and that they have no hope. But Christians resign themselves. They are silent; silence itself is suspicious—even silence is mystery. Why do they not speak out? Why do they not show a natural, an honest indignation? The submitting to calumny is a proof that it is too true. They would set themselves right if they could." [1]

---

[1] *Sermons on Subjects of the Day,* p. 302. Rivingtons, 1869.

Mr. Kingsley, who of all things loved the frank expression of indignation, was scandalized at this apology for self-restraint under misrepresentation,—though our Lord commanded it,—and he treated it as an avowal of Newman's adhesion to the doctrine that truth is no virtue. Of course it was nothing of the kind, and when challenged to produce his proof that Newman had ever said anything of the kind, he made no attempt to support his accusation. He only said that he was very glad to know that Newman had not meant what he seemed to mean, and that he withdrew the imputations. To this Dr. Newman replied by publishing the correspondence, with the following extremely witty summary of its drift.

"Mr. Kingsley begins then by exclaiming, 'Oh, the chicanery, the wholesale fraud, the vile hypocrisy, the conscience-killing tyranny of Rome! We have not far to seek for an evidence of it! There's Father Newman to wit: one living specimen is worth a hundred dead ones. He a Priest, writing of Priests, tells us that lying is never any harm.' I interpose, 'You are taking a most extraordinary liberty with my name. If I have said this, tell me when and where.' Mr. Kingsley replies, 'You said it, Reverend Sir, in a sermon which you preached when a Protestant as vicar of St. Mary's, and published in 1844, and I could read you a very salutary lecture on the effects which that Sermon had at the time on my own opinion of you.' I make answer, 'Oh . . . *Not*, it seems, as a priest speaking of priests; but let us have the passage.' Mr. Kingsley relaxes:—'Do you know I like your *tone*. From your *tone*, I rejoice, greatly rejoice, to be able to believe that you did not mean what you said.' I rejoin, '*Mean* it!

I maintain I never *said* it, whether as a Protestant or as a Catholic.' Mr. Kingsley replies, 'I waive that point.' I object:—' Is it possible ? What ? Waive the main question ? I either said it or I didn't. You have made a monstrous charge against me—direct, distinct, public; you are bound to prove it as directly, as distinctly, as publicly ; or to own you can't !' 'Well,' says Mr. Kingsley, 'if you are quite sure you did not say it, I'll take your word for it, I really will.' My *word !* I am dumb. Somehow I thought that it was my *word* that happened to be on trial. The *word* of a Professor of lying that he does not lie ! But Mr. Kingsley reassures me. 'We are both gentlemen,' he says ; 'I have done as much as one English gentleman can expect from another.' I begin to see: he thought me a gentleman at the very time that he said I taught lying on system. After all it is not I but it is Mr. Kingsley who did not mean what he said. *Habemus confitentem reum.* So we have confessedly come round to this, preaching without practising; the common theme of satirists from Juvenal to Walter Scott. 'I left Baby Charles, and Steenie laying his duty before him,' says King James of the reprobate Dalgarno ; 'O Geordie, jingling Geordie, it was grand to hear Baby Charles laying down the guilt of dissimulation, and Steenie lecturing on the turpitude of incontinence.'"

This summary naturally nettled Mr. Kingsley, and he replied in a pamphlet called *What then does Dr. Newman mean ?* raking up all the evidence he could find that Newman justified, what he has certainly often justified, the guarded and careful mode of doing what Mr. Kingsley might certainly have done in a care-less, headlong, and inpetuous manner, and closing his pamphlet with very bitter remarks on Newman's want of straightforwardness, which virtually amounted to an indictment against the honesty of his whole career. This was the attack to which Newman's *Apologia pro vitâ suâ* was the reply—a book which, I venture to say, has done more to break down the English distrust of Roman Catholics, and to bring about a hearty good fellowship between them and the members of other Churches, than all the rest of the religious literature of our time put together.

I have already made very large use of this singularly frank and straightforward story of the growth of Newman's convictions, on which indeed every student of his life must be dependent for his knowledge of their development. And I do not know that the book requires any further notice here, except in relation to that charge against him of sympathy with indirectness and tortuousness of mind out of which it sprang. As for tortuousness of mind, the charge would now be admitted by all fair judges, to whatever communion they might happen to belong, to be utterly mistaken, as deplorably mistaken as it is well possible for a charge to be. In an appendix to the *Apologia*, Dr. Newman comments on one of Mr. Kingsley's sentences, in which he said, "Dr. Newman takes a seeming pleasure in detailing instances of dishonesty on the part of Catholics," to which Newman replies, "Any one who knows me well will testify that my 'seeming pleasure,' as he calls it, at such things, is just the impatient sensitiveness which relieves itself by a definite delineation of what is so hateful to it."

The number of those persons who "know Dr. Newman well" must have been vastly increased by the publication of the *Apologia*, or the *History of my Religious Opinions*, as it was called in the later editions; and every one of them, I suppose, would heartily concur in this observation of the autobiographer. He is the last man in the world to feel the smallest sympathy with untruthfulness or dishonesty, indeed not to feel the utmost repulsion towards it. A man so genuine in character, so ingenuous in judging himself, has hardly ever made himself known to the world. But though Mr. Kingsley never made a greater mistake than when he discerned any tortuousness of mind in Dr. Newman, his excuse was that Newman's conception of the right mode of getting at truth in religious matters, was undoubtedly what almost all Protestants, and assuredly all Protestants of Mr. Kingsley's rather impatient temperament, would have called eminently complex and indirect. As we have seen, Newman has never found any simple or easily-applied test of truth. He thinks it much easier to believe anything he " ought " to believe, than to find out what truth is without reference to any command or injunction to which he feels it his duty to submit.

His first practical conception of what he " ought " to believe was anything inculcated by Scripture; his next was anything inculcated by the *catena* of Anglican divines, in whom he supposed that he had found the living voice of the Anglican Church. His last and present test of what he ought to believe, is what the voice of the Roman Catholic Church imposes on him; and it is obvious enough that none of these tests, unless it be the last, is very distinct in outline, nor any of them one that admits of off-hand practical application. Newman has never had a supreme confidence in "common-sense," or "instinct," or "intuition," or any other short-cut to religious truth. To him religious truth has been a highly complex problem from the first, not one to be easily solved, but one that, take what test of it he will, requires the greatest care in statement and the utmost precaution in the method of its application. Of his mind, if of any, it has been true, as I said early in this little book, that—

> "The intellectual power through words and things,
> Went sounding on a dim and perilous way."

He has always been disposed to regard the material world as a mere hieroglyphic expression of deeper spiritual meanings. Even in dealing with Scripture, he has from a very early period inclined to mingle the mystical with the more obvious interpretation of the text. And even in accepting the guidance of a Church, he has ever been on his guard against any hasty and inadequate collation of its authoritative definitions. Hence he has vexed all impatient and eager minds, who cut their way to what they deem truth by rough and ready processes, and has laid himself open to the imputation of indirectness. There is a striking instance of this in the celebrated passage in the *Apologia* in which he contrasts the intimate, irresistible, indissoluble connection between belief in self and belief in God, with the mystery of the world as it actually presents itself to us in all its godlessness. "The tokens," he writes, "so faint and broken, of a superintending design, the blind evolution of what turn out to be great powers or truths, the progress of things as if from unreasoning elements, not towards final causes, the greatness and littleness of man, his far-reaching aims, his short duration, the curtain

NEWMAN AS ROMAN CATHOLIC.   233

hung over his futurity, the disappointments of life, the defeat of good, the success of evil, physical pain, mental anguish, the prevalence and intensity of sin, the pervading idolatries, the corruptions, the dreary, hopeless irreligion, that condition of the whole race so fearfully yet exactly described in the Apostle's words, 'having no hope, and without God in the world,'—all this is a vision to dizzy and appal; and inflicts upon the mind the sense of a profound mystery, which is absolutely beyond human solution." [1] It was obvious that a mind which could grasp with such power the paradox of human life in its relation to Divine revelation, could not by any means have presented itself to a vivid and passionate imagination like Mr. Kingsley's as one which he would have called natural and straightforward; and yet its naturalness is naturalness of a very high order, and its straightforwardness as straightforward as any nature so wide and sensitive to all sorts of delicate attractions and repulsions could possibly be. The simplicity of minds such as Newman's, profound as it is, will seem anything but simplicity, will seem complexity, to other men, while the anxious forecast of it will seem artificial.

> "So dark a forethought rolled about his brain,
>   As on a dull day in an Ocean cave,
>   The blind wave feeling round his long sea-hall
>   In silence." [2]

And yet this "dark forethought" is in Newman's case completely overruled and subdued by faith and love.

I feel no doubt that the preparation of the *Apologia*, and the attempt to bring out the course of his own

[1] *Apologia*, pp. 377-8.
[2] *Idylls of the King*, p. 384 of Macmillan's one volume edition.

thought in the long series of changes which at length made him a Roman Catholic, set Newman thinking afresh on the general principles of belief, and led to his attempt to give some general account of those principles in the book published in 1870, which he modestly termed *A Grammar of Assent*. I don't think the title was a very happy one. Whatever the book is, it is not a Grammar of any kind. Instead of dealing with the rationale of language, and the distinctive character of the different parts of speech, its chief endeavour is to show how much there is in the different kinds of assent yielded by the mind to propositions, which cannot be reflected in language at all, and to justify in general the feeling of certitude, even while expressly admitting and contending that that feeling of certitude is often wrongly entertained, and misleading to those who so entertain it.

This is not the place either to analyze or criticize an elaborate and in some respects a technical essay of this kind, but I refer to it for the sake of the light it throws upon the processes of Newman's own mind. I take it that the general drift of the book is to impress on those who read it, that unless the constitution of the human mind may be assumed to be *on the whole* truthful and trustworthy, all attempts to mend it are simply childish. "If I may not assume," he says, "that I exist, and in a particular way, that is, with a particular mental constitution, I have nothing to speculate about, and had better let speculation alone. Such as I am, it is my all; this is my essential standpoint, and must be taken for granted; otherwise thought is but an idle amusement not worth the trouble. There is no medium between using my faculties, as I have them,

and flinging myself upon the external world according
to the random impulse of the moment, as spray upon
the surface of the waves, and simply forgetting that
I am." [1]

As regards belief, Newman shows that man is a believing animal, that he gives credit very easily, and often
of course with very unfortunate results, to what he is
told; but that none the less this credulousness, guarded
as it usually is in its earlier stages by the surroundings
of domestic life, is one of the greatest and most in-
estimable of the preparations and disciplines for life.
"Of the two," he writes, "I would rather have to
maintain that we ought to begin by believing everything that is offered to our acceptance, than that it
is our duty to doubt of everything. This indeed seems
the true way of learning. In that case we soon discover and discard what is contradictory; and error
having always some portion of truth in it, and the truth
having a reality which error has not, we may expect
that when there is an honest purpose and fair talents,
we shall somehow make our way forward, the error
falling off from the mind, and the truth developing and
occupying it." [2] Now as Newman finds that, as a matter
of fact, men are very often certain, and are often rightly
certain, in spite of the fact that they have not unfrequently been wrongly certain, he concludes that certitude
is a reasonable attitude for human nature, and that
though sceptics may try to undermine the feeling of
certitude, they will not succeed. We may do something
in guarding the mind against precipitate and false
certitude, but we shall not root out the confidence that

---

[1] *An Essay towards a Grammar of Assent,* p. 340. Burns, Oates,
& Co., 1870.   [2] *Ibid.* p. 371-2.

on a great number of subjects certitude can and ought to be attained.

"Suppose," he says, "I am walking out in the moonlight, and see dimly the outlines of some figure among the trees;—it is a man. I draw nearer—it is still a man; nearer still, and all hesitation is at an end—I am certain it is a man. But he neither moves nor speaks when I address him; and then I ask myself what can be his purpose in hiding among the trees at such an hour? I come quite close to him and put out my arm. Then I find for certain that what I took for a man is but a singular shadow formed by the falling of the moonlight on the interstices of some branches or their foliage. Am I not to indulge my second certitude because I was wrong in my first? Does not any objection which lies against my second, from the failure of my first, fade away before the evidence on which my second is founded?"[1] Whence Newman concludes, that though we are often certain when we ought not to be, there is plenty of room for true certitude in human life, and that there is room for it even in the case of arguments which, so far as you can make out, appear to afford nothing but a great cumulation of probabilities, from which, speaking *mathematically*, it would be impossible to attain mathematical certainty.

For instance, to a man who has never been in India, it is but an accumulation of testimonies, which may all be unveracious testimonies, that such a place as Calcutta exists. Yet we are all quite certain that it does exist, and justly certain of it. Hence, according to Newman, there is a margin of conviction over and above any

An Essay towards a Grammar of Assent, pp. 223-4.

inferential proof we can give for it in logical form, in most of our legitimate certitudes. And the latter part of his book is occupied in illustrating what he calls the "illative sense," in other words, the power of inferring truth from converging lines of evidence, none of which separately would justify certitude, but all of which, taken together, do justify it, in connection with Christian belief. Newman illustrates the action of what he calls "the illative sense" from the mathematical theory of limits. We know, he says, that the greater the number of the sides of a polygon inscribed in a circle, and the smaller each individual side, the nearer it approaches to the circle itself. Yet as we can never actually deal with a polygon of an infinite number of infinitesimal sides, we have no experience of the truth that such a polygon coincides with the circle. Yet mathematicians do not hesitate to accept as demonstrably true, that what steadily approximates to truth as the limit is approached, is actually true, though we cannot verify its truth, when the limit is actually reached. So it is, in Newman's opinion, with the inference to be drawn from a number of convergent lines of reasoning. Apparently they only accumulate probabilities, and no mere accumulation of probabilites can amount to certainty; yet if a number of different evidences approach the same conclusion from quite different sides of human nature, there is something in the mind which insists on supplementing the formal deficiency in this accumulation of probabilities, and on concluding, so as to inspire certitude, where from the logical point of view there would seem only to be room for a strong presumption. Assent, according to Newman, is an act of the living mind that often passes beyond the formal grounds on which, so far as analysis goes, we can alone consciously justify it. It often concludes peremptorily and even effectually on grounds which, so far as we can draw out explicitly the reasons for our conclusion, would furnish us only with a halting and inadequate argument, just as the living hand and foot will achieve a difficult feat in climbing, of which it would have been impossible beforehand to give the rationale.

It will be seen by what I have said, that Newman's course of thought since he had first joined the Roman Catholic Church had, after a short interval of something like passionate ardour, marked chiefly by the *Sermons addressed to Mixed Congregations* and *Callista*, reverted to its older temper, the temper which discouraged anything like impulsive action, and which placed large faith in time and the gradual effect produced by the implicit action of honest and anxious reflection on an observant and vigilant mind. The *Grammar of Assent*, which is a long plea for cautious and deliberate though courageous reasoning on all the various converging lines of consideration which bear on the Christian revelation, was published in 1870, amidst the excitements of the Vatican Council. It was only natural that Newman, whose heart was more or less identified with his Anglican friends, and with those who had followed in the wake of his Anglican friends, should have been profoundly anxious lest anything done in that Council should retard the movement towards Rome, and drive back men with whose general tendencies of thought he was in sympathy, towards Protestantism or a state of helpless vacillation. I have no doubt that his own mind had long accepted something like the doctrine which was defined at that Council as to the centre of the

Church's infallibility; but he did not think that the time was ripe for so great a step forwards in the way of transforming implicit into explicit doctrine, and he knew that in many cases it would repel hesitating Anglicans, and throw them back on what he called "Religious Liberalism," in other words, the doubt whether there was any final guidance to be had in theology at all.   He was therefore amongst the most earnest of those who were called the "inopportunists," and great was his indignation at the action of Mr. Ward and the *Dublin Review* in urging on the Ultramontanes, and indeed in presenting the doctrine of the infallibility of the Pope, in a form far more extravagant than that which it ultimately took.

A private letter to his Bishop, in which he called these English Vaticanists "an aggressive, insolent faction," was by some breach of faith allowed to creep into print, and for a time the quarrel between the Vaticanists and the Inopportunists in England was extremely hot.   Dr. Newman held that Rome should speak only when some great heresy or other evil impended, and should speak to inspire hope and confidence in the faithful. " But now," he wrote to Bishop Ullathorne, "we have the greatest meeting which ever has been seen, and that at Rome, infusing into us, by the accredited organs of Rome and of its partisans (such as the *Civilta*, the *Armonia*, the *Univers*, and the *Tablet*), little else than fear and dismay. When we are all at rest and have no doubts, and—at least practically, not to say doctrinally—hold the Holy Father to be infallible, suddenly there is thunder in the clear sky, and we are told to prepare for something, we know not what, to try our faith, we know not how. No impending danger is to be averted, but a great difficulty is to be created. Is this the proper work of an Œcumenical Council? As to myself personally, please God, I do not expect any trial at all; but I cannot help suffering with the many souls who are suffering, and I look with anxiety at the prospect of having to defend decisions which may not be difficult to my own private judgment, but may be most difficult to maintain logically in the face of historical facts. What have we done to be treated as the faithful never were treated before? When has a definition *de fide* been a luxury of devotion, and not a stern, painful necessity? Why should an aggressive, insolent faction be allowed 'to make the heart of the just sad whom the Lord hath not made sorrowful'? Why cannot we be let alone, when we have pursued peace and thought no evil?"

Dr. Newman went on to expatiate on "the blight which is falling on the multitude of Anglican ritualists," who were diffusing Church principles far and wide among Protestants, and concluded by saying, "If it is God's will that the Pope's infallibility is defined, then is it God's will to throw back the times and moments of that triumph which He has destined for His Kingdom, and I shall feel I have but to bow my head to His adorable, inscrutable Providence." Oddly enough, considering that he protested thus passionately against the opportuneness of the decree, it was Dr. Newman who was fixed upon a few years later by the general desire of the English Catholics to answer Mr. Gladstone's criticisms on Vaticanism, in that "Letter to the Duke of Norfolk" in which he insisted that there was plenty of freedom left to Catholics, after the Vatican decree, and that that decree in no serious way imperilled the loyalty of English Catholics to the sovereign and laws of England. But the controversy concerning the Vatican decree throws little light on the history of Dr. Newman's own thought, and I shall leave it with the remark that I do not quite understand his question, "Where has a definition *de fide* been a luxury of devotion and not a stern, painful necessity?" Surely the decree on the Immaculate Conception of the Virgin Mary was precisely " a luxury of devotion," and *not* " a stern, painful necessity." Was any great and dangerous heresy repressed by that decree?

The time came, however, when Newman's "minimizing " view of the Vatican definition was once more in the ascendant at Rome. Pius IX. died in 1878, and was succeeded by Leo XIII., who is at least as much a statesman as a theologian. It soon became evident that his policy would be to reconcile the European States with the Vatican, except where they were deliberately bent upon a policy of aggression and persecution, and of course his attention was at once turned to the more eminent men in the different Catholic communities who, while faithful to the Church, had yet regarded his predecessor's policy as premature and unfavourable for the spread of the Roman Catholic faith. Early in 1879 it was known that he wished especially to do honour to his pontificate by numbering Newman among the Cardinals, and Newman, who fully understood that by declining that distinction he should hurt the feelings of all the moderates who had supported him nine years previously, when he was " in disgrace with fortune " and Ultramontanes' eyes, signified his assent. On the sixteenth of April he left Birmingham for Rome, arriving there on the twenty-fourth, and on the twelfth of May, 1879, he received the Cardinal's hat. In his

R

manner of expressing his thanks for the honour conferred on him, the new Cardinal reminded all those who
read his speech of the naturalness, simplicity, and grace
of his old Oxford days. "In a long course of years,"
he said, "I have made many mistakes. I have nothing
of that high perfection which belongs to the writings
of the Saints,—namely, that error could not be found in
them; but what I trust I may claim throughout all I
have written is this—an honest intention, an absence
of private ends, a temper of obedience, a willingness to
be corrected, a dread of error, a desire to serve the Holy
Church, and, through Divine mercy, a fair share of
success." He went on to claim that ever since he
began to take a part in ecclesiastical life at all, he had
opposed what he called "Liberalism in Religion," which
he defined as "the doctrine that there is no positive
truth in religion, but that one creed is as good as
another." It is of course perfectly true that from
the very beginning of his career Newman has been
a steady advocate of what is called dogmatic Christianity, that is, Christianity which is not a formless and
gelatinous mass of vague sentiment, but which springs
from a deeply-planted seed of revealed doctrine, and
has been, in his opinion, developed organically and pro-
videntially from that original germ. But is "Liberalism
in Religion" a happy description of the anti-dogmatic
attitude of mind? I should have thought not. Liberalism
is probably oftener used to signify the disposition to
make concessions to popular demands than in any
other sense, and it is by no means clear that the popular
mind does demand the relaxation of dogmatic restraints
on the Babel-like confusion of religious opinions. In
one sense Newman has been a steady foe of dogmatic

tyranny; virtually he received his Cardinal's hat because he had contended so boldly against any attempt to invade freedom of conscience in the Church. His doctrine has always been that private conscientiousness is the first step towards orthodoxy, and that any attempt to interfere with true liberty of conscience, or even to spur and hurry on its natural pace by external pressure, is in the highest degree dangerous to the cause of true belief. If Newman had never been a Liberal in the sense of making a strong fight for those whose slow conscientious advance was threatened by the despotism of impatient and jealous authority, I do not suppose he would ever have been a Cardinal. In 1870 we witnessed the spectacle of " Blind Authority beating with his staff the child that might have led him." In 1879 Authority, with his eyes couched, raised him who had thus been singled out for the display of ecclesiastical displeasure, to the position of one of the Princes of the Church.

CHAPTER XI.

NEWMAN'S CHIEF POEM, AND THE UNITY OF HIS LIFE.

I HAVE but little left to say of Cardinal Newman, and that little will be best said in connection with his most remarkable poem, *The Dream of Gerontius.* Before the Vatican disputes, and shortly after the close of his controversy with Canon Kingsley, Newman had written a poem of which he himself thought so little, that it was, as I have heard, consigned or doomed to the waste-paper basket; and Mr. Jennings, in his very interesting account of Cardinal Newman,[1] credits the statement. Some friend who had eyes for true poetry rescued it, and was the means therefore of preserving to the world one of the most unique and original of the poems of the present century, as well as that one of all of them which is in every sense the least in sympathy with the temper of the present century, indeed the most completely independent of the *Zeitgeist.*

The Dream of Gerontius is intended to delineate Newman's conception of the last great change through which a faithful Catholic passes, when he exchanges this

[1] *Cardinal Newman, the Story of his Life,* by Henry J. Jennings. Birmingham : Houghton & Company. London : Simpkin & Marshall.

world for the world of spirits. But it is not merely a
poem on death, for it manages to give us in many respects a much more adequate impression of the true
core of Newman's faith and life than any other of his
works. None of his writings engrave more vividly on
his readers the significance of the intensely practical
convictions which have shaped his career. And especially
it impresses on us one of the great secrets of his influence. For Newman has been a sign to this generation,
that unless there is a great deal of the loneliness of death
in life, there can hardly be much of the higher equanimity
of life in death. To my mind, *The Dream of Gerontius* is
the poem of a man to whom the vision of the Christian
revelation has at all times been more real, more potent
to influence action, and more powerful to pre-occupy
the imagination, than all worldly interests put together
—of a man whose whole horizon has been so taken up by
revealed religion that his career embodies a statuesque
unity and fixity of purpose, standing out against our
confused modern world of highly complex and often extremely petty interests, like a lighthouse shining against
blurred and lowering masses of town, and shore, and
harbour, and sea, and sky. *The Dream of Gerontius*,
though an imaginative account of a Catholic's death,
touches all the beliefs and hopes which had been the
mainstay of Newman's life, and the chief subjects of
his waking thoughts and most vivid impressions. It
is impossible to read it without recognizing especially
that Newman had always and steadily conceived life as
a Divine gift held absolutely at God's will, not only in
regard to its duration, but also in regard to the mode
and conditions of its tenure. Death, even to the most
faithful, brings home the thinness of the crust which

R *

separates the personal consciousness from the utter
collapse which follows the withdrawal of God's sustaining power. And death even to the most faithful is the
signal for convincing them of their utter impotence, and
of the constant guardianship of other mightier beings
than ourselves, in the hollow of whose hand we lie as
helpless as the chrysalis in the cocoon of silk. It opens
with a delineation of that "strange innermost abandonment," that "emptying out of each constituent and
natural force," which dismays the soul by fully realizing
to it for the first time its utter incapacity even to cling
fast to that which it supposed to be of its very essence—

> "'Tis death—oh, loving friends, your prayers !—'Tis he.
> As though my very being had given way,
> As though I were no more a substance now,
> And could fall back on nought to be my stay,
> (Help, loving Lord, Thou my sole refuge, Thou),
> And turn nowhither but must needs decay
> And drop from out the universal frame
> Into that shapeless, scopeless, blank abyss,
> That utter nothingness of which I came."

Then the horror of this collapse abates sufficiently for
Gerontius to make his last confession of faith, and give
up his will with hearty fervour to God's ; and then it
returns, and in his dream he dies—but soon awakes to
find himself, as he thinks, refreshed by a strange sleep,
followed by "an inexpressive lightness and a sense of
freedom."

> "I had a dream. Yes, some one softly said
> 'He's gone,' and then a sigh went round the room ;
> And then I surely heard a priestly voice
> Cry *Subvenite;* and they knelt in prayer.
> I seem to hear him still, but thin and low,
> And fainter and more faint the accents come,
> As at an ever-widening interval.

Ah ! whence is this ?   What is this severance ?
This silence pours a solitariness
Into the very essence of my soul ;
And the deep rest, so soothing and so sweet,
Hath something too of sternness and of pain.
For it drives back my thoughts upon their spring
By a strange introversion, and perforce
I now begin to feed upon myself,
Because I have nought else to feed upon.
Am I alive or dead ?   I am not dead,
But in the body still, for I possess
A sort of confidence which clings to me,
That each particular organ holds its place
As heretofore, combining with the rest
Into one symmetry, that wraps me round
And makes me man ; and surely I could move
Did I but will it, every part of me.
And yet I cannot to my sense bring home
By very trial, that I have the power.
'Tis strange ; I cannot stir a hand or foot,
I cannot make my fingers or my lips
By mutual pressure witness each to each,
Nor by the eyelid's instantaneous stroke
Assure myself I have a body still.
Nor do I know my very attitude,
Nor if I stand, or lie, or sit, or kneel.
So much I know, not knowing how I know,
That the vast universe where I have dwelt
Is quitting me, or I am quitting it ;
Or I, or it, is rushing on the wings
Of light or lightning on an onward course,
And we e'en now are million miles apart.
Yet . . . is this peremptory severance
Wrought out in lengthening measurements of space,
Which grow and multiply by speed and time ?
Or am I traversing infinity
By endless sub-division, hurrying back
From finite towards infinitesimal,
Thus dying out of the expansive world ? "

Surely in all literature there has been no more
effective effort to realize the separation of soul and
body, and the thoughts which might possess a soul
separated from the body, than this.   But soon the

spiritual sense opens out. Gerontius becomes aware of
the presence of his guardian angel, in the hollow of
whose hand he is being borne to judgment, and a
conversation ensues in which he is told that in the
immaterial world intervals are no longer measured by
"the swing this way and that of the suspended rod,"
but only by the intensity of the living thought. "It
is thy very energy of thought which keeps thee from
thy God." Then Gerontius becomes aware of evil
beings who are hungering after him, and trying to
renew in him the old spirit of rebellion, and he is told
by his guardian angel that—

> "It is the restless panting of their being ;
> Like beasts of prey, who, caged within their bars,
> In a deep hideous purring have their life,
> And an incessant pacing to and fro."

I know no more powerful conception anywhere of
impotent restiveness and restlessness. Though these
assailants are now impotent, pain is still before the soul
of Gerontius—the pain no longer of temptation and
fear, but of what we may perhaps call the fiery and
purifying despair of love at finding itself so unworthy
of God. The whole scenery of redemption is brought
before Gerontius in the songs of the angels, through
whose hosts he is borne, till at last he hears once more
the prayers of those kneeling around his death-bed,
which are borne into the very presence of God ; and
the Angel of the Agony, who was sent to strengthen
our Lord in Gethsemane, intercedes for the shortening
of this fresh penitent's suffering. Then we learn how
the eager spirit has dashed from the hold of its guardian
angel—

"And, with intemperate energy of love,
Flies to the dear feet of Emmanuel ;
But ere it reach them, the keen sanctity,
Which, with its effluence, like a glory clothes
And circles round the Crucified, has seized,
And scorched, and shrivelled it ; and now it lies
Passive and still before the awful Throne."

The dream virtually ends with this passionate expression of heart-rending anguish and heart-healing hope—

"Take me away, and in the lowest deep
        There let me be,
And there in hope the lone night-watches keep,
        Told out for me.
There, motionless and happy in my pain,
        Lone, not forlorn,—
There will I sing my sad perpetual strain
        Until the morn.
There will I sing and soothe my stricken breast,
        Which ne'er can cease
To throb and pine and languish, till possest
        Of its sole Peace.
There will I sing my absent Lord and Love :—
        Take me away,
That sooner I may rise, and go above,
And see Him in the truth of everlasting day."

The Dream of Gerontius seems to me to contain the happiest summary we could have of the ideal which has pervaded and constituted the significance of the remarkable life I have been trying to review—a life that has fed itself from beginning to end on the substance of Divine revelation, and that has measured the whole length and breadth and depth of human doubt without fascination and without dread—a life at once both severe and tender, both passionate and self-controlled, with more in it perhaps of an ascetic love of suffering than of actual suffering, more of mortification than of unhappiness, more of sensibility and sensitiveness than of actual anguish, but still a lonely and severe and saintly life. No life known to me in the last century of our national history can for a moment compare with it, so far as we can judge of such deep matters, in unity of meaning and constancy of purpose. It has been carved, as it were, out of one solid block of spiritual substance, and though there may be weak and wavering lines here and there in the carving, it is not easy to detect any flaw in the material upon which the long indefatigable labour has been spent.

As I am correcting the last proof-sheets, the news reaches me that the long and gracious life of which I have been writing has suddenly terminated. Cardinal Newman died at the Edgbaston Oratory on Monday, 11th August, 1890, after less than two days' illness, from inflammation of the lungs, and was buried at Rednal by his dear friend Father Ambrose St. John, on Tuesday the 19th. No more impressive testimony could have been afforded to the power, sincerity, and simplicity of the great English Cardinal's life, than the almost unanimous outburst of admiration and reverence from all the English Churches and all the English sects for the man who had certainly caused the defection of a larger number of cultivated Protestants from their Protestant faith, than any other English writer or preacher since the Reformation. Such a phenomenon as this expression of heartfelt English sentiment for a good Roman Catholic would have been impossible a quarter of a century ago; and that it is possible now is due certainly to the direct influence of Cardinal

Newman's life and writings.   And the honour and reverence paid to him are justly due.   In a century in which physical discovery and material well-being have usurped and almost absorbed the admiration of mankind, such a life as that of Cardinal Newman stands out in strange and almost majestic, though singularly graceful and unpretending, contrast to the eager and agitated turmoil of confused passions, hesitating ideals, tentative virtues, and groping philanthropies, amidst which it has been lived.

THE END.

Richard Clay & Sons, Limited, London & Bungay.

18, *Bury Street, W.C., June,* 1890.

MESSRS. METHUEN'S
New Books and Announcements.

METHUEN'S NOVEL SERIES.
THREE SHILLINGS AND SIXPENCE.

Messrs. METHUEN will issue from time to time a Series of copyright Novels, by well-known Authors, handsomely bound, at the above popular price. The first volumes will be :—

F. MABEL ROBINSON.

1. THE PLAN OF CAMPAIGN.

S. BARING GOULD, M.A.,
Author of "Mehalah," &c.

2. JACQUETTA.

Mrs. LEITH ADAMS
(Mrs. DE COURCY LAFFAN).

3. MY LAND OF BEULAH.
(Shortly.)

F. MABEL ROBINSON.

4. DISENCHANTMENT.
(Shortly.)

G. MANVILLE FENN.

5. ELI'S CHILDREN.

S. BARING GOULD, M.A.,
Author of "Mehalah," &c.

6. ARMINELL: A Social Romance.

Other Volumes will be announced in due course.

2

By the Author of "DONOVAN," "WE TWO," &c.

DERRICK VAUGHAN, NOVELIST. By
Edna Lyall. Post 8vo, 2s. 6d. Twenty-fifth Thousand.

"Edna Lyall has not written anything more artistic, or, from the moral point of view, more stimulating. In substance as well as in form, it is the manliest of Edna Lyall's books."—*Academy.*

"This book is likely to be as popular as the rest of this clever writer's books. The sketch is vigorous, and the hero stands on a higher plane than most men. Derrick Vaughan is a very noble fellow. The story is full of interest, and those who read it ought to be better men and women for its perusal."—*Atalanta.*

"We have to express our gratitude for a very beautiful and touching story of a noble life. Edna Lyall's books are like bright stars in the black mass of senseless, useless, and impure fiction with which the book market is being constantly flooded, and her latest work will help to keep her memory green as one of the loftiest-minded novelists of the Victorian Era. It does not seem possible that any one can rise from the perusal of a book like this without feeling more than ever convinced of the existence of something indestructible, eternal, unspeakably beneficent in human nature."—*Sussex Daily News.*

By L. T. MEADE.

A GIRL OF THE PEOPLE. By L. T.
Meade, Author of "Scamp and I," &c. With illustrations by R. Barnes. Crown 8vo, 3s. 6d. [*Shortly.*

By MRS. LYNN LINTON.

ABOUT IRELAND. By E. Lynn Linton.
Crown 8vo. Boards, 1s.

"A brilliant and justly proportioned view of the Irish Question."—*Standard.*

By T. RALEIGH, M.A.

IRISH POLITICS : An Elementary Sketch. By
T. Raleigh, M.A., Fellow of All Souls', Oxford, Author of "Elementary Politics." Fcap. 8vo, paper boards, 1s. ; cloth, 1s. 6d.

"A very clever work."—Mr. Gladstone.

"Unionist as he is, his little book has been publicly praised for its cleverness both by Mr. Gladstone and Mr. Morley. It does, in fact, raise most of the principal points of the Irish controversy, and puts them tersely, lucidly, and in such a way as to strike into the mind of the reader."—*The Speaker.*

"Salient facts and clear expositions in a few sentences packed with meaning. Every one who wishes to have the vital points of Irish politics at his finger's end should get this book by heart."—*Scotsman.*

By F. MABEL ROBINSON.

IRISH HISTORY for ENGLISH READERS.
By F. Mabel Robinson. *Fourth Edition.* Crown 8vo, boards, 1s.

3

UNIVERSITY EXTENSION SERIES.

Under the above title MESSRS. METHUEN will shortly commence the publication of a series of books on historical, literary, and economic subjects, suitable for extension students and home-reading circles. The volumes are intended to assist the lecturer and not to usurp his place. Each volume will be complete in itself, and the subjects will be treated by competent writers in a broad and philosophic spirit. A full list of the series will be issued shortly. The first volume, to be published in August, will be :—

THE INDUSTRIAL HISTORY OF ENGLAND. With Maps and Plans. By H. DE B. GIBBINS, M.A.

EDUCATIONAL WORKS.

BRADFORD SCIENCE SERIES.

Under the above title MESSRS. METHUEN propose to issue a Series of Science Manuals suitable for use in schools. They will be edited by Mr. R. Elliot Steel, M.A., F.C.S., Senior Natural Science Master in Bradford Grammar School, and will be published at a moderate price. The following are in preparation :—

The Elements of Natural Science ... ... Sept., 1890.
Elementary Light and Sound ... ... Oct., 1890.
    „   Electricity and Magnetism ... Oct., 1890.
    „   Heat ... ... Jan., 1891.
    „   Inorganic Chemistry (theoretical).
    „   Practical Physics.
Advanced Inorganic Chemistry (theoretical).
    „   „   „   (practical).

Other Volumes will be announced in due course.

By A. W. VERRALL, M.A.

SELECTIONS FROM HORACE. With Introduction, Notes, and Vocabulary. By A. W. VERRALL, M.A., Fellow and Tutor of Trinity Coll., Cambridge. Fcap. 8vo. *[In the Press.*

By R. E. STEEL, M.A.

PRACTICAL INORGANIC CHEMISTRY. For the Elementary Stage of the South Kensington Examinations in Science and Art. By R. E. STEEL, M.A., Senior Natural Science Master at Bradford Grammar School. Crown 8vo, cloth, 1s. *[Now ready.*

By R. J. MORICH, M.A.

A GERMAN PRIMER. With Exercises. By R. J. MORICH, M.A., Chief Modern
Language Master at Manchester Grammar School. [*In the Press.*

By H. DE B. GIBBINS, M.A.

GERMAN ACCIDENCE. By H. DE B. GIBBINS, M.A., Assistant Master at Notting-
ham High School.

WORKS by A. M. M. STEDMAN, M.A.,

WADHAM COLLEGE, OXON.

FIRST LATIN LESSONS. Fcap. 8vo, 1s.

FIRST LATIN READER. With Notes adapted to the Shorter Latin
Primer and Vocabulary. [*In the Press.*

EASY LATIN PASSAGES FOR UNSEEN TRANSLATION. Fcap.
8vo, 1s. 6d.

EASY LATIN EXERCISES ON THE SYNTAX OF THE SHORTER
AND REVISED LATIN PRIMERS. With Vocabulary. *Second
Edition.* Crown 8vo, 2s. 6d. Issued with the consent of Dr. Kennedy.

NOTANDA QUAEDAM: MISCELLANEOUS LATIN EXERCISES
ON COMMON RULES AND IDIOMS. Fcap. 8vo, 1s. 6d.

LATIN VOCABULARIES FOR REPETITION: arranged according to
Subjects. *Third Edition.* Fcap. 8vo, 1s. 6d.

FIRST GREEK LESSONS. [*In preparation.*

EASY GREEK PASSAGES FOR UNSEEN TRANSLATION.
[*In preparation.*

EASY GREEK EXERCISES ON ELEMENTARY SYNTAX.
[*In preparation.*

GREEK VOCABULARIES FOR REPETITION: arranged according to
Subjects. Fcap. 8vo, 1s. 6d.

GREEK TESTAMENT SELECTIONS. For the use of Schools. *New
Edition.* With Introduction, Notes, and Vocabulary. Fcap. 8vo, 2s. 6d.

FIRST FRENCH LESSONS. [*In the Press.*

EASY FRENCH PASSAGES FOR UNSEEN TRANSLATION.
Fcap. 8vo, 1s. 6d.

EASY FRENCH EXERCISES ON ELEMENTARY SYNTAX.
[*In the Press.*

FRENCH VOCABULARIES FOR REPETITION: arranged according
to Subjects. Fcap. 8vo, 1s.

SCHOOL EXAMINATION SERIES.

EDITED BY A. M. M. STEDMAN, M.A.

Cr. 8vo. 2s. 6d. each.

In use at Eton, Harrow, Winchester, Repton, Cheltenham, Sherborne, Haileybury, Merchant Taylors, Manchester, &c.

FRENCH EXAMINATION PAPERS IN MISCELLANEOUS GRAMMAR AND IDIOMS. By A. M. M. STEDMAN, M.A. *Fourth Edition.*

A KEY, issued to Tutors and Private Students only, to be had on application to the Publishers. Cr. 8vo. 5s.

LATIN EXAMINATION PAPERS IN MISCELLANEOUS GRAMMAR AND IDIOMS. By A. M. M. STEDMAN, M.A. *Second Edition.* KEY (issued as above), 6s.

GREEK EXAMINATION PAPERS IN MISCELLANEOUS GRAMMAR AND IDIOMS. By A. M. M. STEDMAN, M.A. *Second Edition.*
[KEY. *In the Press.*

GERMAN EXAMINATION PAPERS IN MISCELLANEOUS GRAMMAR AND IDIOMS. By R. J. MORICH, Manchester Grammar School. *Second Edition.* KEY (issued as above), 5s.

HISTORY AND GEOGRAPHY EXAMINATION PAPERS. By C. H. SPENCE, M.A., Clifton College.

SCIENCE EXAMINATION PAPERS. By R. E. STEEL, M.A., F.C.S., Chief Natural Science Master, Bradford Grammar School. In three volumes.

Part I. Chemistry.
Part II. Physics (Sound, Light, Heat, Magnetism, Electricity).
Part III. Biology and Geology. *In preparation.*

GENERAL KNOWLEDGE EXAMINATION PAPERS. By A. M. M. STEDMAN, M.A. [KEY. *In the Press.*

EXAMINATION PAPERS IN BOOK-KEEPING, with Preliminary Exercises. Compiled and arranged by J. T. MEDHURST, F. S. Accts. and Auditors, and Lecturer at City of London College. 3s.

ENGLISH LITERATURE, Questions for Examination in. Chiefly collected from College Papers set at Cambridge. With an Introduction on the Study of English. By the Rev. W. W. SKEAT, Litt.D., LL.D., Professor of Anglo-Saxon at Cambridge University. *Third Edition, Revised.*

ARITHMETIC, Examination Papers. By C. PENDLEBURY, M.A., Senior Mathematical Master, St. Paul's School. KEY, 5s.

7

English Leaders of Religion.

UNDER the above title MESSRS. METHUEN propose to commence in the Autumn the publication of a series of short biographies, free from party bias, of the most prominent leaders of religious life and thought in this and the last century.

Each volume will contain a succinct account and estimate of the career, the influence, and the literary position of the subject of the memoir.

MR. A. M. M. STEDMAN will edit the series, and the following are already arranged—

CARDINAL NEWMAN.	*R. H. Hutton.* [*October.*
JOHN KEBLE.	*W. Lock.*
CHARLES SIMEON.	*H. C. G. Moule.*
BISHOP WILBERFORCE.	*G. W. Daniell.*
JOHN WESLEY.	*J. H. Overton.*
F. D. MAURICE.	*Colonel F. Maurice.*
THOMAS CHALMERS.	*Mrs. Oliphant.*

Other volumes will be announced in due course.